North Carolina

NORTH CAROLINA
BY ROAD

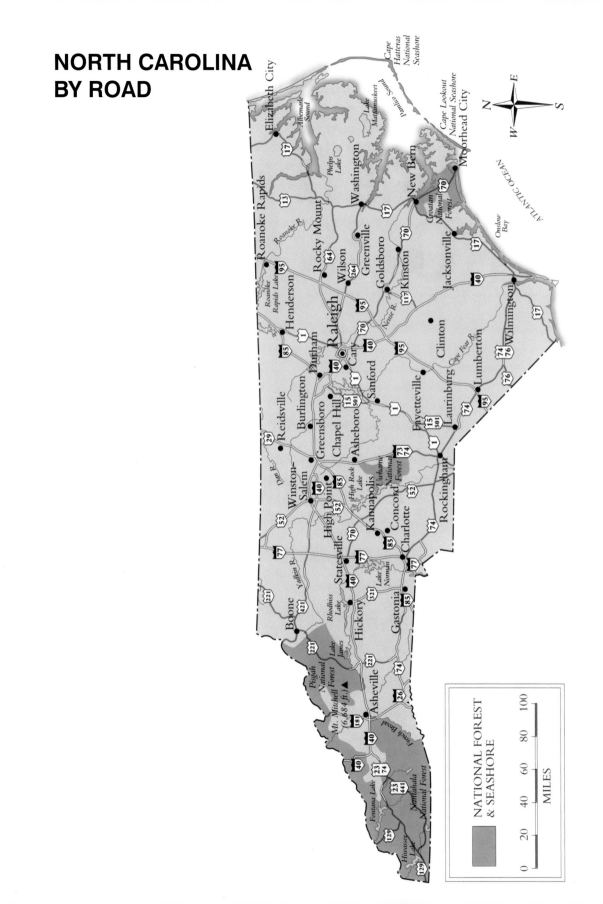

Celebrate the States

North Carolina

David Shirley and Joyce Hart

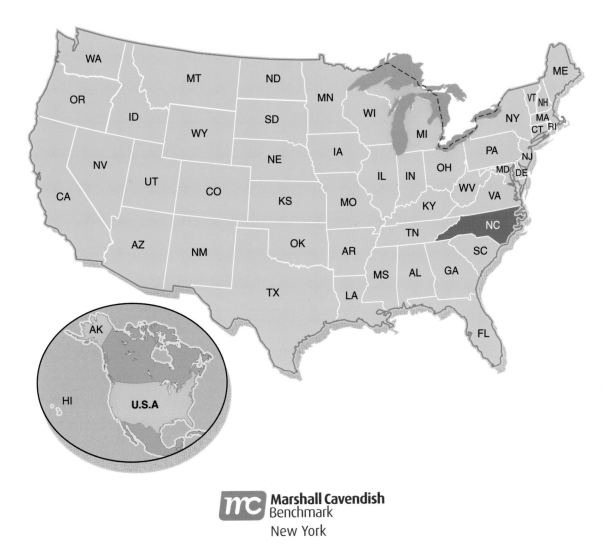

Marshall Cavendish
Benchmark
New York

Other Marshall Cavendish Offices:
Marshall Cavendish Ltd. 5th Floor, 32-38 Saffron Hill, London EC1N 8 FH, UK • Marshall Cavendish International (Asia) Private Limited, 1 New Industrial Road, Singapore 536196 • Marshall Cavendish International (Thailand) Co Ltd. 253 Asoke, 12th Flr, Sukhumvit 21 Road, Klongtoey Nua, Wattana, Bangkok 10110, Thailand • Marshall Cavendish (Malaysia) Sdn Bhd, Times Subang, Lot 46, Subang Hi-Tech Industrial Park, Batu Tiga, 40000 Shah Alam, Selangor Darul Ehsan, Malaysia

Marshall Cavendish is a trademark of Times Publishing Limited

All websites were available and accurate when this book was sent to press.

Library of Congress Cataloging-in-Publication Data

Shirley, David, 1955–
North Carolina / by David Shirley and Joyce Hart.—2nd ed.
p. cm. — (Celebrate the states)
Summary: "Provides comprehensive information on the geography, history, wildlife, governmental structure, economy, cultural diversity, peoples, religion, and landmarks of North Carolina"—Provided by publisher.
Includes bibliographical references and index.
ISBN 978-0-7614-4729-0
1. North Carolina—Juvenile literature. I. Hart, Joyce, 1954– II. Title.

F254.3.S55 2011
975.6—dc22
2009007139

Editor: Christine Florie
Co-Editor: Denise Pangia
Publisher: Michelle Bisson
Art Director: Anahid Hamparian
Series Designer: Adam Mietlowski

Photo research and layout by Marshall Cavendish International (Asia) Private Limited—
Thomas Khoo, Benson Tan and Gu Jing

Cover Photo by Photolibrary/Alamy

The photographs in this book are used by permission and through the courtesy of; *Bes Stock/Alamy*: 21; *Corbis*: 15, 50, 59, 63, 69, 78, 80, 84, 117, 118, 120, 122, 123, 124, 127, 129, 136; *Getty Images*: 52, 66, 70, 119, 121, 126; *National Geographic Image Collection*: 133; *North Wind Picture Archives*: 30, 33, 36, 37, 39, 40; *Photolibrary*: back cover, 8, 12, 19, 20, 22, 23, 24, 27, 45, 47, 72, 86, 90, 92, 98, 102, 105, 108, 109, 134, 135; *Photographer's direct*: 113, 115, 137; *Photolibrary/Alamy*: 14, 16, 18, 25, 28, 54, 56, 74, 94, 96, 97, 100, 101, 112, 128, 130, 131; *Topfoto*: 41.

Printed in Malaysia
1 3 5 6 4 2

Contents

North Carolina Is . . .

It is a place of dreams . . .

In my mind, I'm goin' to Carolina.
Can't you see the sunshine.
Can't you just feel the moonshine.
Ain't it just like a friend of mine
To hit me from behind.
Oh, I'm goin' to Carolina in my mind.

> —from "Carolina in My Mind" by singer James Taylor

. . . and a land of many different scenes, from its beaches . . .

"The most beautiful sight I've ever seen is at the beach at Nags Head. I can just see the foamy blue waves of the Atlantic Ocean lapping up against the white sand. You can crawl up atop the dunes and watch as sheets of sunlight dance across the water and see the strong waves drag the sand back into the sea."

> —a Wake Forest resident

"Attractive Wrightsville Beach is representative of the new communities that have sprung up around boating centers. Drawing its principal sustenance from nearby Wilmington, it is a thriving town of its own now."

> —from *Around America* by Walter Cronkite

. . . to its mountaintops . . .

"Stand at the top of Mount Jefferson, at 4,683 feet, and you'll see the Ashe County Christmas trees, arrayed in dark evergreen smudges on the hills below."

> —from *Far Appalachia: Following the New River North* by Noah Adams

. . . from its small towns and large cities . . .

"I suppose more than anything, it's the way of life in this part of the country that influences my writing. In Eastern North Carolina, with the exception of Wilmington, most people live in small towns."

—author Nicholas Sparks

"It was just another beautiful day in Chapel Hill. As the local saying has it, 'If God isn't a Tar Heel, why is the sky Carolina blue?'"

—from *States of Mind: A Personal Journey Through the Mid-Atlantic* by Jonathan Yardley

. . . or from every corner and everything in between.

"Whether you're looking for adventure or relaxation, mountains or beaches, cities or wilderness, you'll find it in North Carolina!"

—North Carolina Department of Commerce, Division of Tourism

But most of all it is a place where people come together.

"We must remember that North Carolina is more than a collection of regions and people. We are one state, one people, one family, bound by a common concern for each other."

—former North Carolina governor Michael F. Easley

North Carolina is a land of beautiful physical extremes. It has immense mountain peaks, rolling grassy hills, and broad sandy beaches. It is a place where some people celebrate long-held traditions while others pursue the promise of change. In spite of their differences, North Carolinians share a love of the state they have chosen to call home. From the mountains to the beaches, from the city to the countryside, North Carolinians continue to improve their state and the quality of their lives.

Chapter One

The Bluest Skies in the World

From the sandy coastline of the Atlantic Ocean to the towering peaks of the Appalachian Mountains, North Carolina is full of natural wonders and breathtaking beauty. The Atlantic Ocean forms North Carolina's entire eastern border, which stretches for approximately 300 miles. Tennessee sits on its boundary to the west, with South Carolina and Georgia making up its southern border, and Virginia doing the same to the north.

Despite its wide variety of natural landforms, North Carolina is not considered a large state. It ranks twenty-ninth in size among the fifty states, with a landmass of 48,711 square miles. Another way of describing North Carolina is stating that it is 500 miles long at its widest point and 150 miles wide, and is divided into three distinct geological regions.

The Blue Ridge Mountains make up North Carolina's western landscape.

Scientists have classified three different regions that make up the state of North Carolina. Traveling across North Carolina from east to west, the land begins at sea level along the Atlantic Coastal Plain, then slowly rises across the Piedmont Plateau and up to the tops of the Appalachian Mountains.

The Atlantic Coastal Plain

The coastal plain includes both the narrow, sandy shores along the Atlantic Ocean and the broad plains and pine forests that spread nearly 100 miles from the shore toward the center of the state. The eastern portion of the Atlantic Coastal Plain is also referred to as the Tidewater region. The portion that is farther inland is called the Inner Coastal Plain.

The Tidewater section of the Atlantic Coastal Plain contains all the state's Atlantic shoreline as well as the marshland that runs parallel to the coast. This is the area that is most affected by the ocean. Millions of years ago much of this area was underwater. The land in this area is very flat and averages less than 20 feet above sea level.

Farther inland, the Inner Coastal Plain is a combination of rich farmlands and swamps. Many rivers, creeks, and bays dissect the Inner Coastal Plain and in some places spill out across the land and form sprawling swamps and muddy marshlands. The thick trunks of live oak trees and bald cypress rise out of the swampy landscape. On the drier farmland, crops such as peanuts, soybeans, sweet potatoes, and tobacco are grown. Because the Inner Coastal Plain is higher than the Tidewater region, more water is able to drain off it.

At the northeastern corner of the Atlantic Coastal Plain is the Great Dismal Swamp. The swamp lies partly in Virginia and partly in North Carolina and covers more than 111,000 acres of forested wetlands.

LAND AND WATER

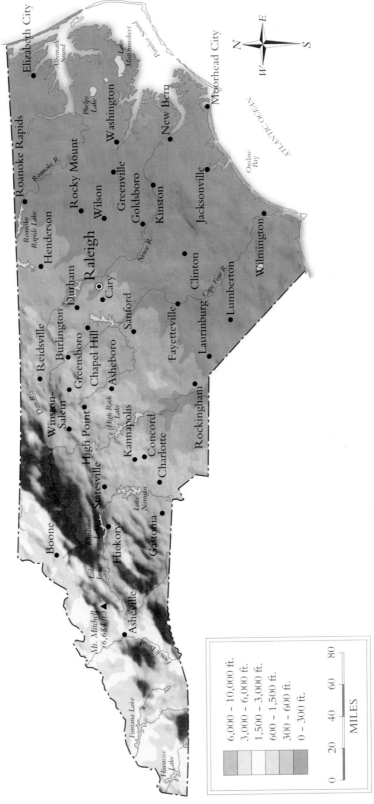

Elizabeth City

Albemarle Sound

Lake Mattamuskeet

Pamlico Sound

Moorhead City

N E S W

ATLANTIC OCEAN

Roanoke Rapids

Phelps Lake

Washington

New Bern

Onslow Bay

Roanoke R.

Rocky Mount

Greenville

Jacksonville

Roanoke Rapids Lake

Henderson

Wilson

Goldsboro

Kinston

Neuse R.

Raleigh

Durham

Cary

Clinton

Lumberton

Wilmington

Cape Fear R.

Reidsville

Burlington

Sanford

Fayetteville

Laurinburg

Dan R.

Greensboro

Chapel Hill

Asheboro

Winston-Salem

High Point

High Rock Lake

Kannapolis

Concord

Rockingham

Statesville

Charlotte

Yadkin R.

Lake Norman

Boone

Rhodhiss Lake

Hickory

Gastonia

Lake James

Mt. Mitchell 6,684 ft. ▲

Asheville

French Broad

Fontana Lake

Hiwassee Lake

6,000 – 10,000 ft.
3,000 – 6,000 ft.
1,500 – 3,000 ft.
600 – 1,500 ft.
300 – 600 ft.
0 – 300 ft.

MILES

0   20   40   60   80

At 37 miles long and 12 miles wide, the Great Dismal Swamp, in northeastern North Carolina, is one of the state's most unique natural wonders of the world.

Though some of the swamp has been drained so settlers could build on the land, much of what is left is unsettled. The great swamp's muddy soil is covered with dense thickets of wild grapes, swamp blackberries, greenbriers, and trumpet vines. Venomous snakes make their homes in the undergrowth. Although a number of roads and bike paths have been cut through the junglelike terrain, the majority of the swamp is difficult to explore on foot. According to local legends the Dismal Swamp is full of the bodies of hunters and hikers who wandered into the dense marshland and never returned. At least these are the stories *some* residents like to tell!

Most of North Carolina's coastline is protected from the strong winds and rough waters of the Atlantic Ocean by a string of sandy reefs and narrow islands known as the Outer Banks. This chain of islands stretches all the way from the state's northern border to Cape

THE LADY OF THE LAKE

The Dismal Swamp is filled with a strange plant called foxfire, which absorbs sunlight during the day and emits an eerie green glow at night. Over the years many legends have arisen as locals have mistaken the glow of foxfire for fantastic creatures ranging from ghosts to flying saucers. Here's one of those legends.

Long ago, a young Indian maiden died a few days before her wedding. After her death the warrior who was to have married her became deeply depressed. He refused to talk to anyone and spent more and more time alone, sitting and walking.

One dark evening the young warrior told his friends that he had seen his lost love paddling a white canoe across the waters of a nearby lake. The young man became obsessed with the idea that the maiden had left her grave and paddled into the darkness of the Dismal Swamp. Each night he walked to the edge of the swamp and waited, as if he expected her to show up. Finally, he left his village for good. His friends believed that he had gone into the swamp in search of her. He was never heard from again.

Jockey's Ridge State Park, located in Nags Head, North Carolina, covers 420 acres and includes some of the tallest natural sand dunes in the eastern United States.

Lookout in the south. The islands of the Outer Banks are prized for their sandy beaches, which run like a brilliant white ribbon between the state's mainland and the Atlantic's blue waters. At Nags Head and Kill Devil Hills the flat beaches rise up dramatically into high sand dunes. The highest of these dunes have colorful names, like Graveyard Hill, Scraggly Oak Hill, and Jockey's Ridge, and offer magnificent views of the ocean to anyone willing to climb them. The islands are separated from the mainland by two large bodies of water, the Albemarle and Pamlico sounds. At some points these sounds are as much as 20 miles wide.

The largest city along North Carolina's eastern coast is Wilmington, which is located near the state's southeastern border. Wilmington is a port city sitting on the Cape Fear River, which flows out to the ocean. More than 99,000 people live in Wilmington, a city that is home to the University of North Carolina at Wilmington as well as Screen Gems Studios, one of the biggest motion picture and television studios outside of Hollywood. Besides the university and the movie studios, Wilmington is a popular tourist destination because the city's location is close to the ocean beaches. Other towns situated on the coastal plain are Jacksonville, Morehead City, and Elizabeth City.

About midway down the coast is the Croatan National Forest, just north of Jacksonville. Croatan is more swamp than forest and is home to

The Croatan National Forest, which covers 159,886 acres of coastal land, offers a variety of habitats that provide excellent homes and safe havens for wildlife.

a large collection of carnivorous plants (plants that eat insects). White-tailed deer, black bear, turkey, squirrel, quail, raccoon, mink, and otter also make their homes there. More commonly seen, though, are the reptiles. Although alligators do live in the swamp, hikers are more likely to spy the snakes, such as cottonmouth moccasins, canebrake rattlers, eastern diamondback rattlers, and copperheads—all of them venomous.

The Piedmont Plateau

The Piedmont Plateau (*piedmont* comes from the French language and means "foothills") stretches down the center of the state from north

At Hanging Rock State Park, Moore's Knob, with an elevation of 2,579 feet above sea level, is a great spot to gaze out at the Piedmont Plateau.

to south. However, the Piedmont Plateau neither begins nor ends in North Carolina. It starts in New Jersey and runs parallel to the Atlantic Coast and the Appalachian Mountains all the way south to Alabama. The Piedmont is about the same size as the Coastal Plain, but its makeup is much different. The Piedmont is a vista of low, rolling hills that range from about 200 feet to about 1,500 feet above sea level. Scientists believe that about 300 million years ago the Piedmont was a mountain range that has, over time, eroded to its present state. The soil of the Piedmont, unlike the soil of the Coastal Plain, is red, claylike, and generally not very fertile.

There are several rivers in this area that are not easily navigated but have been put to work as sources of electricity. Also in this area are rocks that contain gold and other precious metals. Cabarrus County has been given the honor of being called the site of the first U.S. gold rush, which occurred in 1799. Gold miners were still looking for gold there in the 1930s.

Although this portion of North Carolina contains clusters of farms, many of which grow tobacco, the Piedmont is known primarily for its industry and sprawling cities. The five largest cities in the state—Charlotte, Greensboro, Winston-Salem, Durham, and the capital city of Raleigh—are all located in the Piedmont region.

In the Piedmont's southeastern corner are the Sandhills. In contrast to the heavily urbanized northern and western Piedmont, the Sandhills are mostly rural. Grassy hills, peach orchards, and pine forests are much more common in the Sandhills than is the occasional small town. With its vast green meadows, the Sandhills are also a popular place to raise horses.

Charlotte, one of the five largest cities in North Carolina, is located in the Piedmont region.

The Appalachian Mountains

The Appalachian region, which forms the western border of the state, is composed of many connecting mountain ranges, including the Blue Ridge and the Great Smoky mountains. All are part of the Appalachian chain, which stretches from Georgia to Maine. The region is famed for its spectacular fall colors, which come from the changing leaves of a wide variety of trees—more than 120 of them. In fact, the mountains of North Carolina are home to more types of trees than exist in all the countries of Europe combined. The region is the most beautiful in the early morning or just before sunset, when clouds of fog often settle like a smoky blue haze over the dark mountains. The Cherokee Indians, who lived in the area before the first European settlers arrived, referred to the North Carolina mountains as "the place of blue smoke."

Among the most spectacular sites in the region are the towering peaks of Grandfather Mountain and Mount Mitchell, which at

6,684 feet is the highest point in North America east of the Black Hills of South Dakota. There are a total of forty-three peaks in the North Carolina section of the Appalachians that exceed 6,000 feet in elevation. Another eighty-two peaks rise between 5,000 and 6,000 feet. Some of the rocks that make up these mountains are as much as one billion years old. It is in North Carolina that the Appalachians reach their greatest width and elevation. Rising far above the clouds, these majestic peaks provide visitors with panoramic views of the mountain ranges that stretch north and west.

Asheville, a city of more than 73,000 people, is located in the mountainous region of North Carolina. Asheville has gained many nicknames over the years. In 2008 it was named one of the happiest places in the United States to live.

Tourists and residents flock to North Carolina's Great Smoky Mountains to catch a glimpse of the autumn colors.

In addition to its long coastline North Carolina has abundant rivers, streams, and waterfalls. Mountainous western North Carolina is filled with cascading waterfalls, crystal-clear lakes, and cool running streams. In all, the state boasts more than three hundred waterfalls, including Whitewater Falls, which consists of the upper falls, which drops down 411 feet; and the lower falls, which drops down 285 feet. Together, this is the highest set of waterfalls on the East Coast, with a total drop, from top to bottom, of nearly 700 feet. Most of the state's waterfalls are hidden deep in the forests. Hikers can often hear the steady stream of water splashing onto the rocks long before they see them.

The state is also crisscrossed by rivers. The New River, like many other rivers in the region, is narrow, deep, and flows rapidly. There are other rivers, however, that are wide and peaceful. Broad rivers like the Cape Fear and the Neuse rivers provide seagoing vessels with easy access to inland ports.

North Carolina's most spectacular waterway, the Intracoastal, was actually made by human beings. For most of the state's history harsh winds and rough waters were a constant danger for ships sailing from one

The Intracoastal Waterway was constructed during the early twentieth century to provide a navigable route along its length without many of the hazards of travel on the open sea.

Whitewater Falls is a series of waterfalls and cascades on the Whitewater River in North Carolina.

end of the North Carolina coast to the other. The Intracoastal Waterway was constructed during the early twentieth century to provide sailors with a safe passage down the coast in calm waters. The Intracoastal Waterway connects the natural inland waterway between the Outer Banks and the mainland with dozens of rivers, streams, and small lakes, forming one continuous inland canal. Each year the waterway provides smooth sailing for thousands of barges and other commercial and private boats making their way up and down the coast.

TREES AND PLANTS

Along with the dramatic diversity of its terrain, North Carolina provides sightseers with a stunning variety of trees, flowers, and other plants.

Spectacular displays of the Catawba rhododendron can be viewed from late May to late June at Roan Mountain.

The dense mix of red spruce, Fraser fir, hemlock, and tulip poplars that crowd the mountains' lower slopes give them a deep bluish green hue. All along the mountainsides purple mountain laurel, orange flame azalea, and pink Catawba rhododendron provide splashes of color.

The hillsides of the Piedmont are filled with huge oak and hickory trees, which tower above the red maple, dogwoods, and sourwoods that crowd the lowlands. To the south the wooded areas of the Sandhills are dominated by longleaf pines. Throughout the Piedmont grows an astonishing variety of wildflowers, often in dazzling, multicolored combinations. Among the more common are the brilliant orange blossoms of the daylily, the tiny purple buds of the blazing star, and the full red petals of the Shirley poppy.

The warm, damp weather and sandy shores of the coastal plain and barrier islands create an ideal environment for oaks, loblolly pine, and insect-eating plants, such as the Venus flytrap and the pitcher plant. The sweet nectar that coats the inside of the pitcher plant's deep, funnel-shaped leaf attracts wasps and bees. Once inside, the insect slides down the full length of the leaf to its base, where it drowns in a pool of liquid.

The pitcher plant is a carnivorous plant whose prey-trapping mechanism features a deep cavity filled with liquid known as a pitfall trap.

Animal life also varies widely from one end of the state to the other. The dense mountain forests of western North Carolina are home to beavers, bobcats, boars, and black bears. Mountain hawks soar high above the trees. North Carolina's mountains are also an ideal place to find salamanders. In fact, more species of salamanders live in the region than anywhere else in North America. The giant spotted salamander known as the hellbender can be seen scurrying near the entrances of caves or resting on shaded, moss-covered stones.

Many woodpeckers and hawks nest in the Piedmont's woods. The area's meadows and farmlands are filled with bobwhite quails

Hellbenders, found in the rugged mountains of North Carolina, are one of the largest salamanders in the world, growing to over 2 feet long.

THE RED WOLF

The shy red wolf is one of the scarcest species in North Carolina. With its reddish brown fur and black streaks, it is also one of the most attractive. The red wolf originally lived throughout the southeastern United States. By the 1960s, however, hunting and land development had driven the wolves from their homes. Fortunately, scientists were able to keep a few of the animals alive in captivity until they could find somewhere for them to live. The red wolf was declared extinct in the wild in 1980.

The red wolf was reintroduced to North Carolina in 1987. At that time four pairs were released into the marshland of the Alligator River National Wildlife Refuge. The area was chosen for its warm weather and the absence of hunters and land development. The area was also ideal because the white-tailed deer, raccoon, and other small animals that live there would provide the wolves with abundant prey.

After the wolves were released, they quickly began to reproduce. As soon as a newly born red wolf is located, it is outfitted with a radio transmitter. This enables scientists to keep track of its whereabouts and safety. So far the project has been extremely successful. Today only 100 to 120 red wolves are known to exist in the wild. Of these, 83 live among the forests and marshlands around Alligator River.

and cardinals, North Carolina's state bird. Wild turkey, white-tailed deer, raccoon, fox squirrel, and scarlet king snakes are also common in the region.

The Piedmont's many wildflowers attract a colorful array of butterflies. On summer afternoons bright butterflies, such as the painted lady and the tiger swallowtail, flit lazily from flower to flower. And on summer evenings streetlights attract an astonishing assortment of gigantic moths, including the deep green Pandora sphinx and the yellow and orange imperial moth. The most breathtaking of these enormous insects is the rare, pale green luna moth, which can sometimes be seen along the state's roadsides and forest paths.

The coastal plain and barrier islands provide habitats for an incredible variety of birds. More than four hundred species live along the Outer Banks alone, with another one thousand species migrating along the coastline each spring and fall. Osprey, tern, pelican, and barn owl are among the more common birds found in the area. The ocean waters off the North Carolina shore are filled with life, including loggerhead turtle, humpback whale, dolphin, and such tropical fish as mahimahi and wahoo.

PERFECT WEATHER

With its long, mild summers and clear blue skies, North Carolina is a popular destination for tourists in search of warm beaches, calm mountain lakes, and all types of outdoor recreation. The average high temperature is 90 degrees Fahrenheit during July and August. The average low temperature during December and January varies from 28 °F in Asheville, in the mountains, to 40 °F in Wilmington, on the coast.

In some areas of North Carolina, populations of the luna moth are declining due to habitat change.

The Outer Banks, along North Carolina's eastern shore, are vulnerable to the high winds and strong surf caused by hurricanes.

North Carolina receives a generous amount of rain and snow during the year. The southwestern hills receive 75 inches of both rain and snow a year, while the northwestern mountains receive only 40 inches. Across the state the heaviest rain occurs during the hot days of July and August. Average snowfall varies dramatically from one region to another, with up to 30 inches in the mountains and usually less than 2 inches along the shore.

In spite of its generally pleasant weather conditions, North Carolina can occasionally be forced to endure the extreme. Most of the time the Outer Banks protects the rest of the state from the powerful storms that strike between June and November. Hurricane Hugo hit in 1989, with 100-mile-per-hour winds. This unusually fierce storm traveled from the coast, more than 200 miles inland, causing destruction as far as the foothills on the mountains. In the late 1990s violent weather struck the shore with even greater force than usual. As with Hurricane Hugo, several major storms blew across the barrier islands and onto the mainland. One of the most destructive storms was Hurricane Fran, which pounded the area around Cape Fear with 115-mile-per-hour winds in 1996. By the time the storm lifted, it had caused more than $1 billion in damage. An even stronger storm, Hurricane Isabel, with 145-mile-per-hour winds, hit the state in 2003. Then in 2004 Hurricane Charley packed winds measuring 125 miles per hour.

Despite weathering some extremes, North Carolina is best known for the calm weather that follows the storms and the blue skies that provide the backdrop for the state's stunning landscapes. Although there is no scientific evidence to support their claims, many North Carolinians say that, on clear days, their state has the bluest skies in the world.

Chapter Two

Protest and Prosperity

Throughout its history North Carolina has been prosperous. In its earliest years the region's abundant natural resources made North Carolina an attractive place to settle. More recently the inventiveness and hard work of its residents have helped the state continue to thrive, but great sacrifices and protests have sometimes been required to bring prosperity and freedom to all.

THE ANCIENT PEOPLE

During the Paleo-Indian period, from 10,000 to 8000 BCE, nomadic hunters and gatherers roamed the area that is now North Carolina. Great glaciers still covered some of the ground, and these ancient people lived by hunting now-extinct animals such as the mastodon, which provided them with meat as well as skins from which to make clothing and shelter.

The people referred to as the Archaic Indians came next, sometime between 7000 and 2000 BCE. The glaciers had receded by then, and these

Early pioneers built cabins in the mountains where they raised livestock.

people lived in a climate that is similar to the one North Carolinians enjoy today. The plants and animals differed from those available to the Paleo-Indians, with white-tailed deer becoming a plentiful source of meat. Wild fruit and seeds rounded out the diet of the Archaic Indians. These people were nomadic, traveling with the seasons in search of food, but they stayed for short periods of time along the many riverbanks that still exist in the area. Archaeologists have found shards of pottery and polished stone tools that they believe were used by this group.

Sometime between 1000 BCE and 1000 CE a different group of people took up residence in North Carolina. This group is known as the Woodland people. The Woodland people lived more settled lives, building villages and leaving behind more sophisticated pottery and tools. They also left behind signs that they were farmers, growing such plants as sunflowers and marsh elder. The plants they raised did not supply all the nutrition they required, however, so these people continued to hunt animals and to gather wild foods.

Members of the Mississippian culture followed, living in the region from about 800 CE until the 1500s. During this period people from three major language groups made their homes in what is now North Carolina. This means there were three major languages spoken among the native people living in the area when Europeans first arrived. These were the Algonquian language, whose speakers lived mostly on the Coastal Plain; the Iroquoian, whose speakers lived on the Inner Coastal Plain and in the western mountains; and Siouan, whose speakers lived in the Piedmont area. Today the Cherokee are an Iroquoian-speaking tribe; the Saponi speak a Siouan language; and the Lumbee speak various languages.

Corn was one of the major crops grown by American Indians in North Carolina.

When Europeans arrived, they found that many of these tribal people grew different crops on their farmlands, with corn being one of the major ones. Beans and squash were also important crops. The native people are also said to have introduced tobacco to the Europeans. Hunting continued to provide a source of nutrition for the native people.

AMERICAN-INDIAN LIFE

In the days before Europeans first sailed into the region, North Carolina was home to about thirty American-Indian groups, including the Tuscarora, the Hatteras, and the Cherokee.

The Tuscarora and the Hatteras were among the tribes that lived in small villages near the ocean or along rivers and streams. Villagers often built walls or dug ditches around their settlements to protect themselves from enemies and predators. They got food by farming, fishing, and hunting with bows and arrows.

The Cherokee lived in small villages in the Appalachian Mountains in what is now western North Carolina. They cut down trees to build homes and canoes and fashioned clothing out of animal hides. The Cherokee used tree bark and the roots, leaves, and berries of plants to make medicines to treat injuries and disease.

EUROPEANS ARRIVE

When the first Europeans arrived in the region that would become North Carolina, there were approximately 35,000 American Indians living there. This was not a known fact to an Italian explorer named Giovanni da Verrazano, who sailed along the mid-Atlantic coastline in 1524. He traveled from the area near the Cape Fear River on the southern shore all the way to the northern corner of what is now North Carolina. During the next fifty years a number of Spanish explorers led expeditions north from Florida into the area of North Carolina, but neither France nor Spain set up a colony there—except for a Spanish outpost at Fort San Juan, established in 1567–1568.

During the 1580s what would later become North Carolina's coastline became the site of England's first colonies in the New World. Sir Walter Raleigh, who had been granted the land by Queen Elizabeth I, sent two expeditions to the area. Little is known about the first settlement. It was established on Roanoke Island in 1585 and quickly failed.

TALKING TO THE ANIMALS

Telling stories has always been a sacred part of Cherokee life. Here is a tale explaining how the world came to be.

Long ago, humans and animals lived together as friends. Each night they sat around the campfire and told stories. The snakes talked about the things they saw while crawling through caves. The wolves told about life in the valleys and clearings. The bears shared their adventures while hunting for honey along the mountainsides. And the human beings talked about making pots and building houses in the villages.

As the years passed the people began to spend more time talking about their own lives—and less time listening to the animals' stories. "They never hear anything I have to say," hissed the snake. "All they want to do is hear themselves talk," howled the wolf. "It's an insult," roared the bear. "Let's leave here and never come back!" None of the humans heard what the animals said. They were much too busy talking to one another. And none of them noticed as the animals left the campsite and wandered off into the woods.

Many years later a large bear walked into the humans' village. "Good morning," said a woman walking by. "Roar," said the bear. "I can't understand you," said the woman. "Let me take you to our chief. I'm sure he'll understand what you have to say." But neither the chief nor anyone else in the village could understand the bear. Finally, the bear wandered back into the woods.

A few days later a young man was chosen to go and live with the animals and learn their language. When he returned to the village many years later, he could hiss like a snake, howl like a wolf, and roar like a bear. He could also share the animals' stories in human words that the other villagers could understand.

Two years later a second group of settlers, led by John White, arrived at Roanoke Island. Shortly after they arrived, a baby girl named Virginia Dare was born. She was the first child born to English-speaking parents in the New World.

The new colonists made their homes in the wooden houses left behind by the first settlers. They quickly made friends with the American Indians who lived in the area. But the settlers had difficulty surviving off the resources available on the island. White soon returned to England to get more food and supplies.

In the 1500s English colonists landed on Roanoke Island.

For almost three years war between England and Spain made it impossible for White to return to the colony. When he finally returned to Roanoke Island in 1591, he discovered that the colony had been abandoned. No trace remained of the settlers he had left behind. The only clue he could find was a single word: *Croatoan*, which was carved in huge letters on a wooden post, and the letters *CRO* carved on a tree.

John White returned to Roanoke Island in 1591 to discover that the English colonists had vanished.

THE SOUTHERN PLANTATION

Not until the 1650s did English settlers finally gain a foothold in the region. During that period a steady flow of settlers from southeastern Virginia moved into the northeast corner of what would become North Carolina.

In 1663 King Charles II of England presented the Province of Carolina as a gift to eight men, called the Lords Proprietors, who had helped him come to power. Their property stretched all the way from Virginia to the Spanish colony of Florida and included much of present-day North and South Carolina.

From the beginning the Lords Proprietors had problems governing the colony. There were frequent arguments with Virginia over land. And a dreaded pirate known as Blackbeard constantly attacked supply ships off the coast. But the most serious conflict was with the Tuscarora, the native people who lived along the Neuse River. Chief Hancock of the Tuscarora was angry with the white settlers for building homes and farms on his tribe's land. In 1711 the Indians attacked an English settlement near present-day New Bern, killing hundreds of people. During the next year the Europeans and the Tuscarora fought one battle after another. After their defeat, the Tuscarora fled north to New York.

In 1729 all but one of the Lords Proprietors sold their land back to the English Crown. As a result North Carolina and South Carolina became Crown colonies. North Carolina was governed by the same laws in place under the Lords Proprietors, but now it was the British king who appointed the governor and other colonial officials.

SLAVERY AND THE QUAKERS

During the 1740s and 1750s a group of English settlers known as the Quakers moved from Pennsylvania into the Piedmont region of North Carolina. Most settled near what would become Greensboro. Then, in 1753, a German religious group called the Moravians founded the village of Salem. In the following years waves of German settlers from Pennsylvania migrated into the area, building sawmills, tanneries, and small breweries. The Quakers and the Moravians believed that everyone should have the right to worship in any way they pleased. They also believed that all people—regardless of the color of their skin—were equal in the eyes of God.

African slaves had first arrived in North Carolina with the earliest European explorers and settlers. As large tobacco and cotton plantations sprang up along the southern coast and around Charlotte, more and more slaves were brought into the region. Slaves worked from sunrise to sunset each day, clearing the land and planting and picking crops.

Visiting North Carolina in 1747, the Quaker missionary John Woolman was deeply troubled by the conditions under which the slaves lived and worked. "I saw so many vices and corruptions increased by this slave trade and this way of life," he wrote, "that it appeared to me as a dark gloominess hanging over the land." Through his preaching and writing, Woolman convinced many Quaker settlers to free their slaves and to speak out against slavery.

Slave labor used in the cotton fields helped to build economic wealth for the early colonists.

A NEW NATION, A NEW STATE

As the years passed, North Carolinians came to resent being ruled by William Tryon, a governor they had not elected. In western North Carolina a group calling themselves the Regulators began to openly protest British rule of the colony. In 1775 people in western North Carolina expressed their desire to be free from England. The movement for independence soon spread all across the colony. On July 15, 1775, North Carolina's last colonial governor, Josiah Martin, returned to

England on a British warship after he was chased from the colony by a group of angry patriots. Eight years later, at the end of the Revolutionary War, North Carolina found itself part of a new nation. On November 21, 1789, North Carolina representatives signed and ratified the new U.S. Constitution and thus became the twelfth of the original thirteen states.

In 1828 former North Carolina resident Andrew Jackson was elected U.S. president. One of the young nation's most celebrated military leaders, Jackson had become a national hero during the War of 1812. He was also known for his campaign against the Creek and Seminole Indians. While president he drove the native

North Carolina colonials celebrated the Declaration of Independence in 1776.

people farther and farther west. Later, in 1838, President Martin Van Buren ordered U.S. troops to remove the Cherokee from their homes in western North Carolina, fulfilling Jackson's plan to clear the area of the American Indians. The Cherokee were forced to relocate, mostly on foot, to a reservation in Oklahoma. Suffering from cold, disease, and starvation, many Cherokee died during the thousand-mile journey that became known as the Trail of Tears. But hundreds of Cherokee

American Indians were forced to leave their land and to march along what is now called the Trail of Tears, which took them to land west of North Carolina.

avoided capture by hiding in the forests and later escaped into the North Carolina mountains, where their descendants continue to live.

THE CIVIL WAR

By the 1850s slavery had already begun to disappear in North Carolina. There were very few slaves in the mountains or along the coast. In the Piedmont, where slavery was more common, the Quakers and Moravians had convinced many of their neighbors to free their slaves.

ON THE AFFAIR BETWEEN THE REBEL GENERALS HOWE AND GADDESDEN

During the American Revolution North Carolina–born general Robert Howe was put in command of the southern Continental forces. His appointment was met with great disapproval in South Carolina. Howe was unpopular there due in part to his bitter rivalry with South Carolina's general Christopher Gadsden (spelled differently in the song). The situation got so out of hand that the two actually fought a duel—which, though bloodless, calmed things down between them.

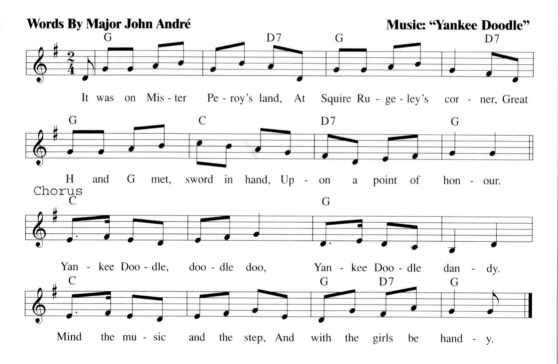

Words By Major John André

Music: "Yankee Doodle"

It was on Mis - ter Pe - roy's land, At Squire Ru - ge - ley's cor - ner, Great H and G met, sword in hand, Up - on a point of hon - our.

Chorus

Yan - kee Doo - dle, doo - dle doo, Yan - kee Doo - dle dan - dy. Mind the mu - sic and the step, And with the girls be hand - y.

They met, and in the usual way,
With hat in hand saluted,
Which was, no doubt, to shoe how they
Like Gentleman disputed *Chorus*

And then they both made
This honest declaration,
That they came there—by honor led,
But—not by inclination. *Chorus*

That if they fought, 'twas not because
Of rancour, spite or passion,
But only to obey the laws
Of custom and of fashion. *Chorus*

The pistols then, before their eyes,
Were fairly prim'd and loaded!
H wish'd, and so did G likewise,
The custom was exploded. *Chorus*

But as they now had gone so far
In such a bloody business,
For action straight they both prepar'd
With—mutual forgiveness. *Chorus*

Quoth H to G—Sir, please to fire,
Quoth G—no pray begin, Sir;
And truly, one must needs admire
The temper they were in, Sir! *Chorus*

We'll fire both at once, said he,
And so they both presented;
No answer was returned by G,
But silence, Sir, consented. *Chorus*

They paus'd a while, these gallant foes,
By turns politely grinning,
Till after many cons and pros,
H made a brisk beginning. *Chorus*

He miss'd his mark, but not his aim,
The shot was well directed;
It sav'd them both from hurt and shame;
What more could be expected! *Chorus*

Then G, to show he meant no harm,
But hated jars and jangles,
His pistol fired, across his arm,
From H—almost at angles. *Chorus*

H now was call'd upon by G
To fire another shot, Sir,
He smil'd, and,— "after this," quoth he,
"No, truly, I cannot, Sir." *Chorus*

Such honour they did both display,
They highly were commended;
And thus, in sort, this gallant fray
Without mischance was ended. *Chorus*

No fresh dispute, we may suppose,
Will e'er by them be started,
For now the Chiefs, no longer foes,
Shook hands, and—so they parted. *Chorus*

Members of these religious groups had also become leaders in the Underground Railroad, a string of hiding places where runaway slaves could stay on their way to freedom in the North.

In 1861 the long-simmering dispute between northern and southern states over slavery and the division of power between the federal and state governments erupted into civil war. When the war began, the majority of North Carolinians still supported the Union. But when President Abraham Lincoln commanded the North Carolina militia to fight against rebellious troops in South Carolina, North Carolina's position quickly changed. Whatever their feelings about slavery, most North Carolinians were not willing to go to war against their southern neighbors. "I can be no party to this wicked violation of the Constitution," said Governor John Willis Ellis, in defiance of Lincoln's orders. "You can get no troops from North Carolina."

The North Carolina legislature soon voted to secede from the Union and join the other slaveholding states in the newly formed Confederate States of America. Over the next four years the state supplied more than 125,000 men to the Confederate army—more than any other state. North Carolina also suffered three times as many casualties as any other state. On April 26, 1865, Confederate general Joseph E. Johnston surrendered to Union general William Tecumseh Sherman near Durham. It was the last major battle of the Civil War, also known as the War Between the States.

THE WAR'S AFTERMATH

On April 15, 1865, President Abraham Lincoln was killed by an assassin's bullet. Vice President Andrew Johnson, a North Carolina native, was

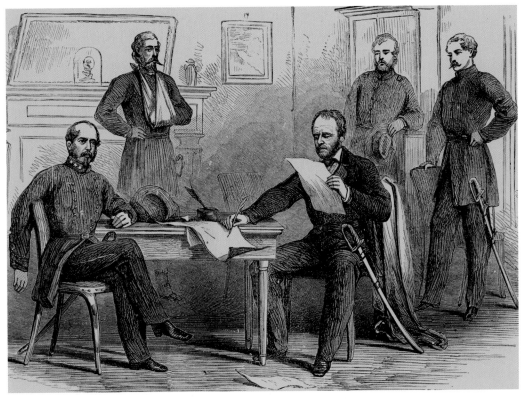

On April 26, 1865, Confederate general Joseph E. Johnston (left) surrendered to Union general William Tecumseh Sherman (middle).

sworn in as president. Johnson attempted to restore the nation to unity, but many northern politicians resented his forgiving stance toward the South. In 1868 the U.S. House of Representatives voted that Johnson should face impeachment—a trial held by the U.S. Senate to determine whether he should be removed from office. Although the Senate did not vote to remove Johnson, he will forever be remembered as the first president to face possible impeachment.

In a curious twist of fate the Civil War contributed to the long-term development of North Carolina's economy. Throughout the war soldiers were given chewing tobacco along with food. Many of these men had never used tobacco before, but once they had tried it, they continued to buy it after the war. With all the new tobacco buyers, tobacco farming and production became a serious business in North Carolina. In 1874 Washington Duke and his sons built their first tobacco factory in Durham. The following year, R. J. Reynolds founded his own tobacco company in Winston-Salem. In the decades that followed, North Carolina would become one of the world's leading tobacco producers.

After gaining their freedom, most former slaves decided to remain in the state. Many continued to work on the small farms and plantations of their former masters. Others took jobs working on tobacco farms or in tobacco factories. But while jobs were plentiful for the freed slaves, life was hard, and their freedom was severely limited. During the 1870s laws known as the Black Codes were passed by the all-white state legislature. These laws prevented African Americans from holding office or owning property. African Americans in North Carolina would continue to suffer under these laws for almost one hundred years.

MOVING FORWARD

During the twentieth century North Carolinians had to overcome hardship and conflict to improve the quality of life in their state. In 1901 Governor Charles B. Aycock formed North Carolina's first public school system. At the time most people in the state worked on farms,

FIRST IN FLIGHT

In 1900 two brothers from Dayton, Ohio, named Orville and Wilbur Wright began trying to build the world's first motorized flying machine. To get their winged inventions off the ground, the Wright brothers wanted to find a location with the best wind conditions for flying. After a lengthy search, they chose a sandy, isolated area called Kitty Hawk, in northeastern North Carolina. In 1900 and 1901 they tested their early glider designs there, both with and without a pilot on board.

In 1902 the brothers successfully tested an improved glider design, sailing 620 feet over the sandy dunes. The following year they returned to Kitty Hawk. This time the glider sported a front-end propeller that was powered by a four-cylinder, twelve-horsepower engine. On December 17 Wilbur tried unsuccessfully to get the new machine off the ground at Kill Devil Hills, a few miles from Kitty Hawk. A few

minutes later Orville gave the machine a second try. It was a success. The whole trip lasted only twelve seconds, and the primitive airplane traveled only 120 feet before it came back to the ground. But the Wright brothers had proved—once and for all—that humans could use motorized machines to fly through the air. The age of air travel had officially begun.

and most school-age children spent almost nine months of the year working alongside their parents, harvesting tobacco, corn, or cotton. Only one out of three children attended school at all. Over the next few decades hundreds of new schools were built and thousands of new teachers were hired throughout the state. North Carolina slowly began to transform itself from a largely illiterate state to a leader in education and literacy in the Southeast.

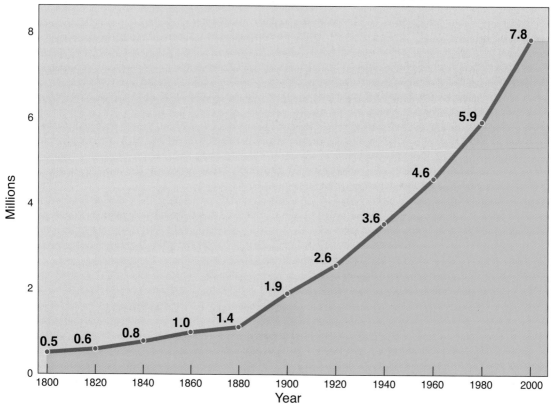

POPULATION GROWTH: 1800–2000

During the 1920s North Carolina began a pioneering road-building program. The hundreds of dirt roads that crisscrossed the state were gradually paved. The new program earned North Carolina the nickname the "Good Roads State." Thanks to this program even today the state has the second-largest system of state-maintained roads in the nation.

In the late 1920s the nation's economy collapsed in what is known as the Great Depression. People were left without jobs or money as businesses shut down and farm prices dropped. North Carolina suffered along with the rest of the nation.

This was an important time of growth for the state, though, as the federal government stepped in with construction projects to put people back to work. Along the coast thousands of North Carolinians were employed digging the canals that formed the Intracoastal Waterway. Meanwhile, workers in western North Carolina built two important routes through the mountains. Begun in the early 1930s, the Blue Ridge Parkway provides millions of travelers with breathtaking views of the North Carolina mountains each year. And the scenic mountain pathways of the Appalachian Trail, which was completed in 1933, help make the Smoky and Blue Ridge mountains among the most popular vacation areas in the nation.

THE CIVIL RIGHTS MOVEMENT

For many years North Carolina's growing prosperity did not extend to all its citizens. Almost one hundred years after the Civil War, African Americans still did not enjoy the same rights and freedoms as their white neighbors.

In 1960 four African-American college students in Greensboro staged a protest that would change life in North Carolina forever. At the

Peaceful protests by African Americans in the 1960s eventually lead to the Civil Rights Act, which outlawed racial segregation.

time most white-owned restaurants in the state refused to serve blacks. The teenagers decided to challenge the practice. On February 1 they sat down at the lunch counter of the Woolworth store in downtown Greensboro and asked to see menus, but the Woolworth employees refused.

The young men, however, refused to leave their seats. During the days that followed, more and more people joined the group—including several white students from the area. This form of protest, called a sit-in, soon spread to other restaurants and stores. A few days later, with television cameras rolling, the young people were finally served their meals. After that, white-owned businesses throughout the state began to open their doors to black customers. "I was tired of just talking about equal rights," Franklin McCain, one of the students, remembered many years later. "This is my country. No one's going to deny me the opportunity. I'm going to be a full participant of every aspect of this community." Similar demonstrations throughout the rest of the South helped to bring attention to the mistreatment and discrimination against African Americans, thus promoting the passage of the Civil Rights Act of 1964.

The ongoing struggle for racial equality in North Carolina has not always been peaceful. In 1971 African-American students were protesting segregation, or the separation of races, in Wilmington schools. After a grocery store was burned down, ten young people were arrested. Many people believed that the teenagers, who became known as the Wilmington Ten, were innocent and had been named as suspects only because of their involvement in the protests. All ten were convicted, however, and received prison sentences of at least twenty years. But in 1976 the three main witnesses against them confessed that they had lied. Four years later the Wilmington Ten were released from prison.

In the early 1970s the once solidly Democratic state started voting more and more with the Republican Party. In 1973 James E. Holshouser Jr. became the first Republican to be elected governor in eighty years.

After the 1972 election of Jesse Helms to the U.S. Senate, North Carolinians sent their first Republican senator to Washington, D.C., since 1903. Helms would go on to spread his conservative influence over the state until he retired in 2003.

MARCHING INTO THE TWENTY-FIRST CENTURY

By 2009 life in North Carolina was changing in many ways. The state, along with the rest of the county, was suffering from a severe economic downturn. There were mass layoffs in almost every industry, leaving many North Carolinians unemployed. The state government was forced to make budget cuts in numerous departments. Things were also changing on the political front. In 2008 North Carolinians had voted for a Democrat, Barack Obama, for U.S. president for the first time in decades. And for the first time in its history North Carolina was being run by a female governor.

In January 2009 Beverly Perdue moved into the executive mansion after being sworn in as governor. Perdue had been the first female lieutenant governor before she won 50 percent of

In 2009 Beverly Perdue was elected the first female governor of North Carolina.

the vote in a tight race for governor. Perdue was not the only woman in the state government. She joined five other women: Secretary of State Elaine Marshall, Treasurer Janet Cowell, Auditor Beth Wood, Superintendent of Public Instruction June Atkinson, and Labor Commissioner Cherie Berry.

As some things changed, others stayed the same. Despite getting hit with a few big hurricanes in the early years of the twenty-first century and a big snowstorm in 2009, North Carolinians can still expect pleasant weather for the greater part of each year. Though tobacco sales were sliding, North Carolina's countryside was still dotted with the familiar and picturesque tobacco barns that people have grown used to seeing. Trips to the state's shoreline continued to bring relief from the hot, sticky days of August. But most of all, no matter what challenge people might have to face, they still love living in this beautiful and diverse state.

Chapter Three

Diversity and More— The People of North Carolina

In 2008 the estimated population of North Carolina was 9,222,414, and this number is steadily increasing. North Carolina had risen to the rank of tenth most populous state in the Union. The rate of population increase, more than 14 percent, makes North Carolina one of the fastest-growing states.

One factor contributing to this growth is the region's favorable living conditions. People from across the country are anxious to become North Carolinians to take advantage of the state's jobs, fair weather, and low cost of living. The largest group of immigrants comes from Mexico and Central and South America. In recent years new immigrants from India

North Carolina's population is one of diversity.

and Southeast Asia have brought the sounds of new languages and the sights of new cultures to the mix of people populating the state.

Much of North Carolina's population is concentrated around the growing urban centers in the Piedmont area, especially such cities as Raleigh and Charlotte, which are rapidly expanding. In 2008 the capital city of the state, Raleigh, had a population close to 380,000, making it the second-largest city in the state and the forty-eighth-largest city in the United States. Charlotte, the largest city in North Carolina, has an estimated 671,588 residents, making it the seventeenth-largest city in the nation. North Carolina's population is estimated to be around

Raleigh is the second most populous city in North Carolina.

ETHNIC NORTH CAROLINA

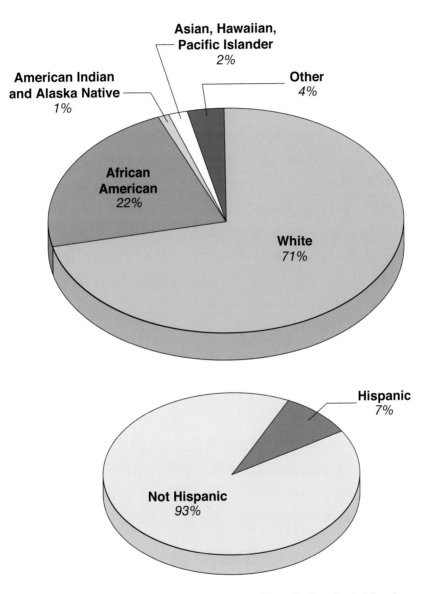

Asian, Hawaiian,
Pacific Islander
2%

American Indian
and Alaska Native
1%

Other
4%

African
American
22%

White
71%

Hispanic
7%

Not Hispanic
93%

Note: A person of Cuban, Mexican, Puerto Rican, South or Central American,
or other Spanish culture or origin, regardless of race, is defined as Hispanic.

71 percent white and about 22 percent African American. Other major population groups include people of Hispanic, Asian, and American-Indian descent.

COMPETITIVE NATURE BRINGS PEOPLE TOGETHER

North Carolinians have always loved competition. The state's athletes often perform at a level that inspires fans from around the state and beyond. But competition in North Carolina extends far beyond the sporting arena. The state is famous for its bluegrass music festivals, in which talented instrumentalists take turns performing solos with the same fierce intensity as prizefighters.

North Carolina's competitive spirit also extends into public life, in debates about everything from politics to religion. This competitive spirit can help onlookers recognize and appreciate the diversity of North Carolina's people.

SPORTS

From basketball to baseball, football, tennis, soccer, and much more, there are few things that North Carolinians care more about than sports. And the state is home to many different types of sport fans and athletes. For instance, Lee and Richard Petty, father and son from Randolph County, dominated stock car racing for more than three decades. That is one reason the state is filled with racing fans, who have for many years followed the careers of the Pettys as well as other local racers.

With North Carolina's mild year-round temperatures and its rolling hills, the state is home to magnificent golf courses, which are popular destinations for golfers from around the world. The meadows of the

One of the more popular outdoor spectator sports in North Carolina is car racing.

Sandhills boast more than forty golf courses, including the Pinehurst Country Club, where the prestigious U.S. Open golf tournament is sometimes held.

Since the Carolina Panthers came to Charlotte in 1995, North Carolinians have been developing an enthusiasm for professional football. Though they struggled in their first few years, the Panthers, members of the National Football Conference, made it to the Super Bowl in 2004, where they lost to the New England Patriots.

One of the biggest sports attractions in North Carolina, however, is college basketball. In recent years five different North Carolina colleges have made the National Collegiate Athletic Association (NCAA) tournament, which determines the best team in college basketball.

For many decades residents of the state have been divided by the heated competition between North Carolina's two most successful teams—the Duke Blue Devils and the University of North Carolina at Chapel Hill Tar Heels. These two teams have had more than their share of outstanding players, but the real heroes in Carolina basketball have been the coaches. During the 1980s and 1990s Chapel Hill's Dean Smith and Duke's Mike Krzyzewski were probably the two most popular and respected men in the state and among the most revered in college basketball across the country. Almost every year during those decades one of the coaches led his team to the Final Four, in which the nation's top four teams compete for the championship. Smith's team won two national championships before he retired in 1997, with a blazing record of 879 career wins that has yet to be topped. Krzyzewski's team has won three championships. Krzyzewski remains an active coach, and in 2008

POPULATION DENSITY

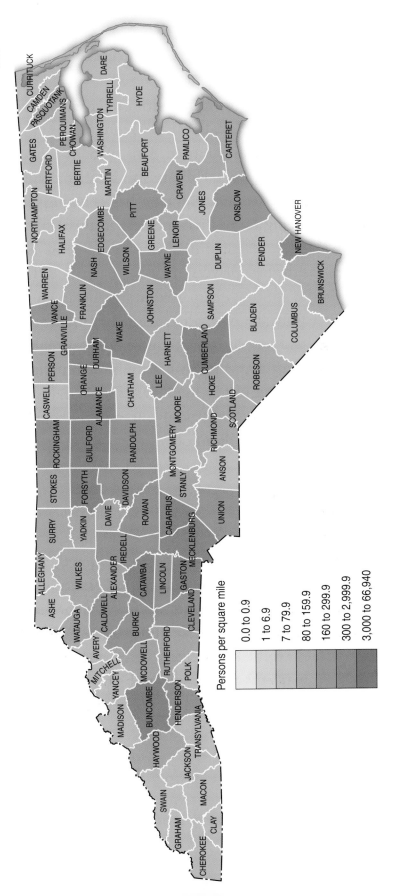

CURRITUCK
CAMDEN
PASQUOTANK
PERQUIMANS
CHOWAN
DARE
GATES
HERTFORD
BERTIE
WASHINGTON
TYRRELL
HYDE
NORTHAMPTON
MARTIN
BEAUFORT
CARTERET
HALIFAX
EDGECOMBE
PITT
PAMLICO
WARREN
NASH
WILSON
GREENE
CRAVEN
JONES
ONSLOW
NEW HANOVER
VANCE
FRANKLIN
LENOIR
DUPLIN
PENDER
GRANVILLE
WAKE
JOHNSTON
WAYNE
SAMPSON
BRUNSWICK
PERSON
DURHAM
LEE
HARNETT
CUMBERLAND
BLADEN
COLUMBUS
CASWELL
ORANGE
CHATHAM
MOORE
HOKE
ALAMANCE
MONTGOMERY
SCOTLAND
ROCKINGHAM
GUILFORD
RANDOLPH
RICHMOND
ROBESON
STOKES
FORSYTH
DAVIDSON
STANLY
ANSON
SURRY
YADKIN
DAVIE
ROWAN
CABARRUS
UNION
ALLEGHANY
WILKES
ALEXANDER
IREDELL
MECKLENBURG
ASHE
CALDWELL
CATAWBA
LINCOLN
GASTON
WATAUGA
BURKE
RUTHERFORD
POLK
CLEVELAND
AVERY
MITCHELL
MCDOWELL
YANCEY
MADISON
BUNCOMBE
HENDERSON
TRANSYLVANIA
HAYWOOD
JACKSON
SWAIN
MACON
GRAHAM
CLAY
CHEROKEE

Persons per square mile

0.0 to 0.9
1 to 6.9
7 to 79.9
80 to 159.9
160 to 299.9
300 to 2,999.9
3,000 to 66,940

he recorded his eight-hundredth career win. It remains to be seen if he will match or even beat Smith's record.

Even with Smith retired, fans of both Duke and the University of North Carolina basketball are still bitterly divided. Each spring people throughout the state find themselves cheering passionately for one team while cheering just as passionately against the other. Family members and close friends get into heated arguments about which of the two teams has the best players, the best coach, and the best fans. "There's just no middle ground when it comes to Duke and Carolina," explained a minister from the Asheville area who is a devoted Tar Heel fan. "People hate one and love the other. During the tournament especially, you'll see sane, responsible people, who are normally kind and respectful of one another, rooting just as loudly for the other team to lose as they do for their own team to win. And if you want me to be honest about it, I'm the same way. It's really kind of embarrassing if you think about it."

RELIGION

Religion is central to the lives of many North Carolinians. The vast majority of the state's citizens are Christian, and most of them can be seen heading to services each Sunday morning, dressed in their finest clothing. The best-known religious leader in the United States during the past forty years, the Southern Baptist minister Billy Graham, makes his home in the tiny mountain town of Montreat, about 20 miles south of Asheville.

While North Carolinians agree about the importance of religion in their lives, they often disagree about what they believe. People in rural parts of the state tend to be conservative in their religious beliefs.

For many North Carolinians, participation in some form of organized religion is an important part of life.

Most conservative Protestants, called Fundamentalists, believe that the Bible is literally true and that there is only one way to interpret it. They also believe that the Bible should be taught in public schools and that men—not women—should be leaders in the church, the family, and society at large. "What we believe may not be popular with everyone," said a conservative minister in Winston-Salem. "But the Bible teaches what it teaches, and it's important that everyone has the chance to hear it."

Christians in the Piedmont and in urban areas and college towns tend to be more moderate or liberal in their religious beliefs. Moderate Christians believe that the Bible can be interpreted in different ways. They believe that personal religious beliefs should not be practiced in schools and that women should join in as leaders in all areas of life. "For me, it's less about quoting a particular passage from the Bible and more about living my life in the spirit that the Bible reveals," said a Raleigh resident. "I think if we spent less time arguing about what the Bible says and more time living what it teaches, the world would be a much better place."

Through the years conservative and moderate Christians in North Carolina have disagreed over a number of issues. On several occasions Baptist leaders have challenged Wake Forest University, which was founded by Southern Baptists, for having certain policies, such as allowing alcohol to be served on campus. One of the more bitter controversies involved Southeastern Baptist Theological Seminary in Wake Forest. In the early 1980s Fundamentalists took control of the board of trustees of the traditionally moderate seminary. Within a few years almost all the faculty members had been replaced with more conservative teachers.

"The thing about being from North Carolina," explained a Southeastern Seminary graduate, "is that no matter how much you may disagree with someone, you still have a common ground as fellow North Carolinians. I think that's what's different about what happened at Southeastern. Once the new people took over, there wasn't any room to disagree any more. But I suspect that will change one day soon. We here in North Carolina have strong opinions and we often disagree with each other, but we somehow always seem to find that common ground."

Of course, there are other religious groups that practice their faith in North Carolina. Though the groups are smaller in number, their presence is felt. Charlotte has a large community of people of the Jewish faith who meet at the large campus of Shalom Park. With increased immigration from India and Asia, there are also great numbers of Muslims and Hindus living in the state, especially around the metropolitan areas, such as Raleigh.

BLUEGRASS AND BEACH MUSIC

Music is another thing North Carolinians feel strongly about—and are opinionated about as well. For people in the western part of the state the traditional music, called bluegrass, is often the music of choice. Bluegrass music began in Kentucky in 1938, when mandolin player Bill Monroe formed his band, the Blue Grass Boys. As perfected by Monroe, bluegrass combines the mournful melodies of the African-American blues with the lyrics and instrumental styles of traditional Irish, Scottish, and English folk music. From its earliest days bluegrass was characterized by the astonishing skill and blistering speed of the musicians who played it.

Bluegrass may have gotten its start in Kentucky, but the mountain people of western North Carolina quickly put their own stamp on it. In the years before bluegrass was developed, Spray native Charlie Poole developed a new style of banjo playing—by plucking the instrument one note at a time with his fingers—that would later have an enormous impact on the genre. Flint Hill native Earl Scruggs took Charlie Poole's banjo technique and turned it into an art form. In the 1950s Doc Watson, a blind musician from the tiny township of Stoney Fork, transformed the guitar from a rhythm instrument into a solo instrument with a new

The music of choice for many westerners in North Carolina is bluegrass, often played by Doc Watson at folk music festivals.

style of playing called flat-picking. "I tell you," said an accountant from Asheville, "seeing Doc Watson on stage is something you're never likely to forget. . . . It's total concentration and absolute joy. He shuts his eyes tight and his head rocks into the rhythm of the song—and those fingers of his move so fast across the face of that guitar that you can hardly see them anymore. If you love music, there's just nothing like it anywhere."

Today, bluegrass is still very much alive in North Carolina. Each spring and summer thousands of people attend bluegrass festivals all across the state. But the granddaddy of bluegrass festivals—in North Carolina or anywhere else—is the Ole Time Fiddler's and Bluegrass Festival, which is held in the sleepy little community of Union Grove.

EASTERN NORTH CAROLINA BARBECUE SAUCE

The most important thing about barbecue sauce is finding the taste that's right for you. This simple recipe should allow you to add and mix ingredients until you find just the right taste. Have an adult help you with the cooking.

1 quart vinegar
1/4 cup salt
1/2 tablespoon cayenne pepper
1 tablespoon red pepper flakes
1/4 cup packed brown sugar (or 1/2 cup honey)

Stir all the ingredients together. Taste. Add additional pepper, salt, or sugar until it tastes just the way you like it. Let the entire mix stand overnight.

Most North Carolinians prefer their barbecued dishes with very little sauce, but it's really up to you to decide how much—or how little—to use. Cook meat, fish, chicken, tofu, or vegetables over an open grill outdoors. Each time you turn the item over the fire, use a brush or wooden spoon to apply a coating of sauce. Once the food has cooked, add an extra layer of sauce to taste.

Over the years the nation's finest bluegrass musicians have saved their most spirited performances for the fans from around the world who crowd into Union Grove during the last weekend in May. For the more adventurous fans the festival also offers lessons on playing—and making—bluegrass instruments, such as mandolins, guitars, and hammer dulcimers.

At the other end of the state, people living along the shore spend their springs and summers listening—and dancing—to another type of music. Locals call it beach music. The beach music tradition began during the early 1970s, when a smooth style of African-American music called rhythm and blues became popular at dances and beach parties. To local beachcombers the music's soft, shuffling rhythms seemed perfect for dancing the shag barefoot in the sand in the moonlight. Before long local bands filled out their sets with classic rhythm-and-blues tunes from the 1950s and 1960s, and local songwriters began writing new songs with the same smooth rhythms and wistful lyrics as the old ones. Soon visitors were coming to the area just to hear the music.

NORTH CAROLINA'S FAVORITE FOOD

North Carolina's most enduring contribution to American cooking is its unique style of pit-cooked pork barbecue. To achieve the distinctive taste and smell, a pig is roasted in a deep pit over a wood or charcoal flame. The meat is lightly covered with a sauce, which is usually made with vinegar, hot peppers, and sugar.

Almost everyone in the state has an opinion about how to make the best barbecue. Most North Carolinians have little patience for outsiders who prefer the meat cooked in other barbecue hotbeds such as Texas or Memphis, Tennessee. "There's only one way to make barbecue,"

Family and friends barbecuing some of their favorite foods.

boasts a factory foreman from Zebulon, "and that's the way we make it here. Who do people think they're kidding with all that heavy sauce they put on their meat? If the meat is cooked right, there's no need to cover it. You just give it a little seasoning to bring out the flavor, and it's ready to eat just like it is."

In fact, North Carolinians themselves tend to disagree, both about how the pork should be cooked and the sauce that should be used to flavor it. Barbecue eaters near the coast prefer to cook the whole pig at once and to baste it with a sharp vinegar and pepper sauce that contains no tomatoes. As you move farther west, people tend to cook only the shoulders of the hog and to soften their sauce by adding a light tomato paste to the mix.

"UNTO THESE HILLS"

In 1950 a group of businessmen decided the mountainous area of southwestern North Carolina needed a financial boost. They put together a play they thought would attract tourists to the area. And they were more successful than they had dreamed. "Unto These Hills" portrays the history of the Cherokee people from the mid–1500s until 1838, when many of them were forced by federal troops to walk from North Carolina to the lands of present-day Oklahoma in a journey now known as the Trail of Tears.

Today the same dramatization continues to attract visitors to the 2,800-seat Mountainside Theatre in Cherokee, North Carolina. "Unto These Hills" is a play staged outdoors about the Cherokee people, who have lived in those mountains for thousands of years. Through this dramatization audiences are told of the tribe's unique history; the Cherokee lived by a democratic government, established a written language, and knew how to read. The play also tells of the hardships the Cherokee endured during the Trail of Tears. Those who refused to leave hid in the forests and were later granted a small portion of their ancestral land, which once stretched throughout much of the Southeast. The performance includes traditional costumes and dance. One of the heroes of this play is Sequoyah, the Cherokee man who created the Cherokee alphabet.

The idea of barbecuing an entire hog at once became popular in the city of Lexington. Each Saturday afternoon folks would gather around to watch and wait as two large pigs were slowly barbecued over an open pit dug in the center of the town square. Eventually, the pit was moved inside a wooden shelter with a brick chimney, with a restaurant right beside it. Barbecue restaurants are still usually small, no-nonsense places, with paper plates and simple wooden tables. And Lexington is still the most popular place in North Carolina to eat barbecue.

AMERICAN-INDIAN CULTURE

When white people first came to the area that is now North Carolina, there were several tribes of American Indians living there. Although their numbers have decreased over the centuries, American Indians in North Carolina still boast a thriving culture.

There are several tribes spread throughout the state. Groups of American Indians live in such places as Clinton, Hollister, Pembroke, Winton, Mebane, Cherokee, and Bolton. They are members of the Coharie, Cherokee, Lumbee, Meherrin, Waccamaw Siouan, and Saponi tribes. North Carolina is home to one of the largest populations of American Indians on the East Coast. Today their estimated population stands at around 110,000.

The population of North Carolina contains descendants of the region's first inhabitants as well as the most recent immigrants. The cultures and beliefs of the population also represent the full range of ideas and preferences. Though some discussions might explode into loud public debate, North Carolina is quickly becoming a more interesting state because of the differences inherent in its people. Most residents agree that this beautiful southern state is a great place to live.

Chapter Four

Government for All, Even When Divided

Politics have always been explosive in North Carolina. People often disagree sharply over how the state should be governed. For almost one hundred years after the Civil War, Democrats controlled politics in North Carolina. In the late 1960s some Democrats took strong stands in favor of greater rights for African Americans and against the Vietnam War. At the same time, many of the state's more conservative citizens—particularly those from small towns and rural areas—began to speak out against the views of the Democratic Party.

Over time, conservative North Carolinians began voting for Republican candidates in greater and greater numbers. Today the state is evenly divided between urban centers like Charlotte, Raleigh, and Winston-Salem—where Democrats are still the majority—and the

North Carolina's Capitol, completed in 1840, provides office space for the governor, lieutenant governor, and their administrative staff.

primarily Republican rural areas and small towns. Together, these two political parties have ruled the state, coming together through compromise while continuing to compete in the political arena.

North Carolina's government is divided into three branches: executive, legislative, and judicial.

Executive

The governor heads North Carolina's executive branch. He or she is responsible for appointing important officials and introducing new policies in such areas as education, health care, and law enforcement. The governor is elected to a four-year term. Other officials in North Carolina's executive branch include the lieutenant governor, the state treasurer, and the attorney general.

Elected government officials meet in the legislative building to pass new laws for the state.

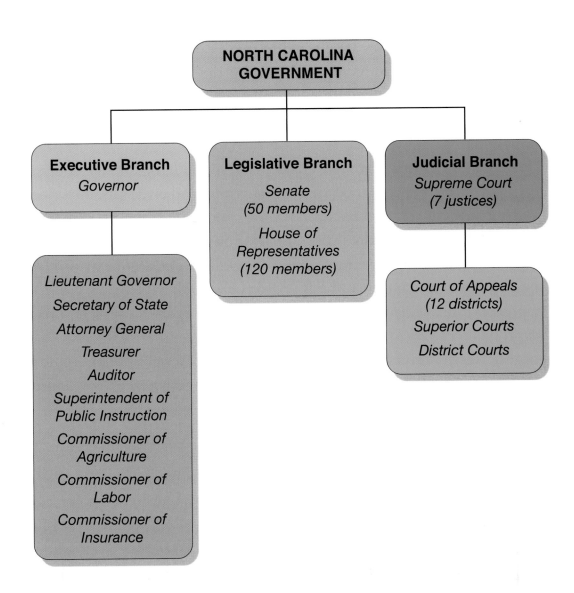

NORTH CAROLINA GOVERNMENT

Executive Branch
Governor

Lieutenant Governor
Secretary of State
Attorney General
Treasurer
Auditor
Superintendent of Public Instruction
Commissioner of Agriculture
Commissioner of Labor
Commissioner of Insurance

Legislative Branch
Senate (50 members)
House of Representatives (120 members)

Judicial Branch
Supreme Court (7 justices)

Court of Appeals (12 districts)
Superior Courts
District Courts

Legislative

The North Carolina legislature is divided into two houses: a senate with 50 members and a house of representatives with 120 members.

Members of both houses are elected to two-year terms. The legislature is responsible for introducing and passing the bills that will become state laws. After a majority of the members in both houses pass a bill, it is signed by the governor and becomes law.

Judicial

Most trials in North Carolina are held in superior or district courts. District courts hear cases involving minor crimes and civil suits. Superior courts try more serious cases. Whenever someone disagrees with the decision of one of the state's trial courts, the case is sent to the court of appeals to decide whether the decision should be upheld or overruled. If the decision of the court of appeals is also challenged, the North Carolina Supreme Court, the state's highest court, reviews the case. It has the final say in the matter.

All North Carolina judges are elected. The seven supreme court justices, twelve court of appeals judges, and all superior court judges are elected to eight-year terms. District court judges serve four-year terms.

DEMOCRATS, REPUBLICANS, AND THE HISTORIC 2008 PRESIDENTIAL ELECTION

Race plays an important role in the lives of North Carolina's citizens. Most people—both black and white—agree that North Carolina has made great strides since the 1960s in providing freedom and opportunity for its people. However, black and white North Carolinians have had a much harder time learning to get along on a personal level. One of the biggest problems has been where people live. Most African Americans live in the Piedmont region and the northern coastal plain. Meanwhile, people who live in the western mountains are almost exclusively white.

NORTH CAROLINA
BY COUNTY

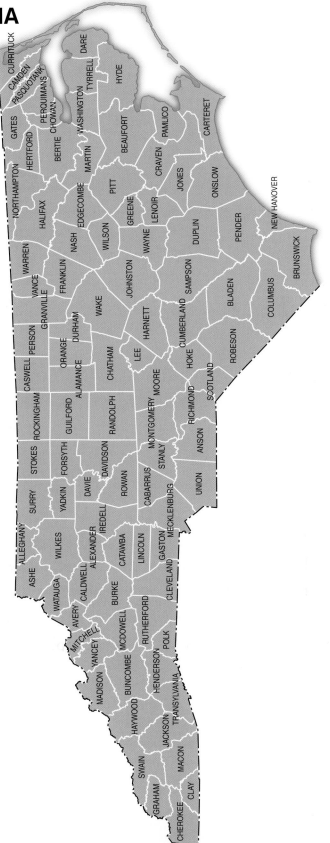

YEAR-ROUND SCHOOLS

Race is not the only issue about which people in the state argue. A heated debate about many North Carolina counties switching from traditional school calendars, which allow students at least two months off during the summer, to year-round schools has been taken all the way to the state's supreme court. In December 2008 the seven state justices heard arguments from people on both sides of the issue.

A group of parents from Wake County filed a suit against its school district because they felt their rights had been taken away when they were not asked if they wanted their children to participate in the year-round school schedule. With a year-round schedule, students attend school for nine weeks, then have a three-week break. This nine weeks on, three weeks off schedule can be disruptive for a family, especially if both parents are working. However, the year-round schedule helps school districts accommodate the rapidly increasing student population without having to build more schools. With a year-round schedule one group of students is always in attendance. With the traditional schedule all children are on vacation at the same time, leaving the schools empty during the summer.

Studies have shown that students do at least as well in a year-round school setting as they do in a traditional one. However, some parents are outraged that they have no decision-making powers as to which academic calendar their children will follow. The justices have heard arguments from both sides, but it may be a year or more before they make their decision. While the justices deliberate, parents and school districts continue their debate.

Because of this geographic separation some pockets of the black and white populations of North Carolina have very little contact with each other. This lack of contact sometimes leads to misunderstanding and suspicion.

In recent years blacks and whites have often found themselves on opposite sides of political debates. While most whites in the state regularly vote Republican, African Americans are much more likely to vote Democratic.

Until the reelection of George W. Bush, who won the state in the 2004 presidential election with 56 percent of the vote, North Carolinians typically upheld their Republican reputation. In the 2008 election, however, a record-breaking turnout of North Carolina voters, both black and white, helped to elect Barack Obama, the country's first African-American president. It was a very close race in North Carolina; Obama won by fewer than 20,000 votes. It was the first time in more than thirty years that North Carolinians voted for a Democratic presidential candidate. North Carolina was considered a pivotal state in the 2008 election. The state's electoral votes helped the Democratic candidate cinch the win.

Chapter Five

The Economy— From Farms and Factories to Services

Like all the other states in the Union, in 2008 and 2009 North Carolina's economy was hit by failing banks, rampant bankruptcies, and high unemployment. Across the economic spectrum, from finance companies to technology-based firms, agricultural products, and textile industries, 2008 and 2009 were not good years. The unemployment rate at the beginning of 2009 was 8.7 percent, one of the highest in all the states and the highest in North Carolina since 1983.

The recession, plus the effects of the globalized marketplace, led economists to see the state's evolving economy as a good thing. The economy had been moving away from one based on agriculture

Each year North Carolina raises about 45 percent of the nation's tobacco crop, which is the largest production in the country.

and manufacturing toward a more service-based one. Service industries are businesses that serve people. This includes technological research companies, as are found in Raleigh's Research Triangle Park, as well as finance companies, insurance businesses, retail stores, restaurants, and other businesses that help people in one way or another, as opposed to making products.

AGRICULTURE

Agriculture is one of the oldest industries in the state. It dominated North Carolina's economy until the end of the nineteenth century.

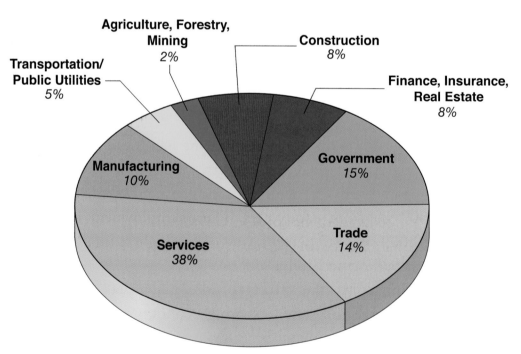

NORTH CAROLINA WORKFORCE

Agriculture, Forestry, Mining 2%

Construction 8%

Transportation/ Public Utilities 5%

Finance, Insurance, Real Estate 8%

Manufacturing 10%

Government 15%

Services 38%

Trade 14%

Despite the emphasis on manufacturing, technology, and service industries, the state's 48,000 farms still play an important role in its economy. Over 150,000 workers are employed on farms, and they help to harvest crops that bring in more than $1.8 billion.

One of the state's chief agricultural products is greenhouse plants, which bring in more than $800 million each year. North Carolina ranks fourth in the United States in greenhouse agriculture. The second-largest agricultural sales are in tobacco. Each year North Carolina raises about 45 percent of the nation's tobacco crop, the largest production in the country, valued at about $409 million. Additionally, North Carolina is first in the nation in the manufacture of cigarettes and other tobacco products. More than half of the cigarettes purchased each year in the United States are produced and packaged in the state. The R. J. Reynolds Tobacco Company in Winston-Salem operates two of the world's largest facilities.

Other crops the state produces include corn, peanuts, cotton, peppers, cucumbers, cabbage, tomatoes, and sweet potatoes. North Carolina farmers produce more sweet potatoes than any other state. Vegetable production overall brings in more than $160 million each year. Christmas trees are another important crop, adding about $100 million to the state's economy each year. North Carolina ranks second in the country in the production of Christmas trees. Another important crop is fruit. North Carolina ranks fourth in the nation in fruit production, which brings in about $80 million annually.

In recent years raising cattle for both beef and dairy products has become increasingly important to the state's economy. Other valuable livestock products are chickens and turkeys. Fishing is another

Christmas trees are an important part of North Carolina's agricultural production.

important source of income in the state, especially in coastal waters. Flounder, sea trout, and croaker are the most popular catches, along with crabs, oysters, clams, and shrimps.

MANUFACTURING

In the early parts of the twentieth century many spinning and weaving mills were built in the state, taking advantage of its swift streams to power them and of the cotton produced in the state. During this time many textile companies from the northern states moved to North Carolina and helped to create a textile industry as the Piedmont area became a center for industrial development in the South. The manufacturing of such textiles as fabric, yarn, thread, and clothing is still an important industry in the state. North Carolina is one of the nation's leaders in textile production.

HAMS AND YAMS

Although North Carolina is no longer the agricultural producer it once was, many people are committed to preserving the memory of the old rural way of life. Smithfield's Ham and Yam Festival is one of the tastiest ways to experience a bit of it. Each year more sweet potatoes (also known as yams) are grown in the fields around Smithfield in Johnston County than anywhere else in the nation. A highlight of the festival is the sweet potato–cooking contest. The sweet potatoes can be prepared however the contestant chooses—baked, sugar-coated, pureed, or french-fried. But whatever the recipe, the sweet potatoes must have been grown in Johnston County.

Johnston County is also famous for its delicious hams. For years the festival has included a contest between cooks in Smithfield and their counterparts in Smithfield, Virginia, to see who can prepare the tastiest ham. Today the ham-cooking contest includes cooks from across North Carolina.

Besides all the good eating, the festival features exhibits about farm life and rural arts and crafts. "It's really a wonderful opportunity to show young people how most of us used to live," said a teacher from Raleigh, who brings her children to the festival each year. "It's something that's so easy to forget. But the taste of that ham and those sweet yams—that's something you'll never forget."

The textile industry in North Carolina is among the strongest in the nation.

As the twenty-first century dawned, however, there were signs that the state's traditional tobacco and textile industries were fading in importance. This does not mean that manufacturing in itself was losing significance, though. According to a report released in 2008 by the North Carolina Chamber of Commerce, "The benefits and economic impact of manufacturing in North Carolina are great—historically and today." North Carolina is the seventh-largest manufacturing state in America, and some people are optimistic about the future, despite the downturn in production the state has experienced. Though the textile, tobacco, and furniture industries are suffering, new development in the pharmaceutical and other chemical-manufacturing industries could boost the economy, some economists believe. Chemical manufacturing creates such things as cleaning products and synthetic fibers.

Other important industries in the state include the manufacture of computers and electronic equipment. The manufacturing of auto parts is also important to the state's economy. Although no cars are produced in North Carolina, individual automobile parts are. One-fourth of the manufacturing sector in North Carolina is tied to the manufacture of cars, trucks, and buses.

2007 GROSS STATE PRODUCT: $399 Million

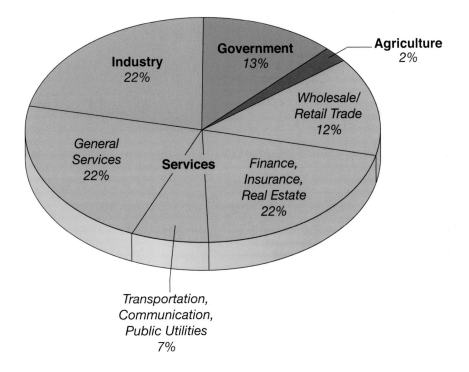

EARNING A LIVING

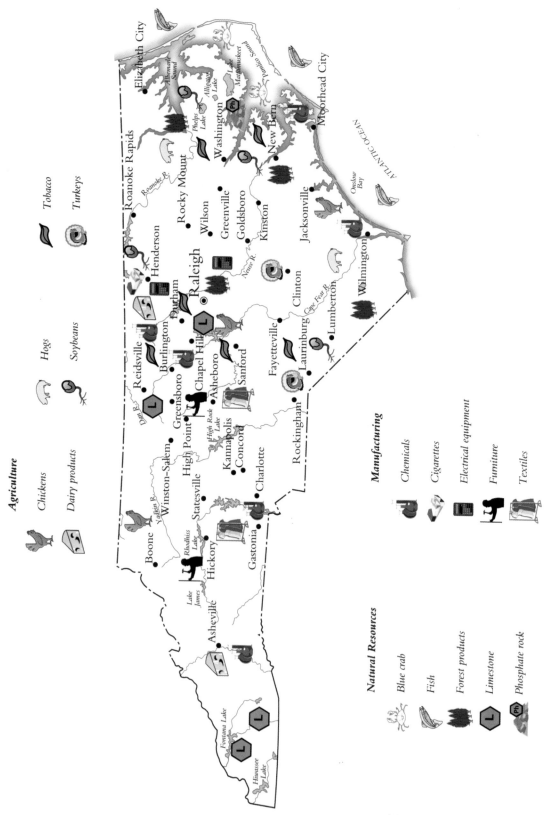

Agriculture
Chickens
Dairy products
Hogs
Soybeans
Tobacco
Turkeys

Manufacturing
Chemicals
Cigarettes
Electrical equipment
Furniture
Textiles

Natural Resources
Blue crab
Fish
Forest products
Limestone
Phosphate rock

SERVICE INDUSTRY

About 70 percent of North Carolina's economy is based on the service industry. The largest players include financial institutions (banks), insurance companies, and real estate developers. Next in order of importance are businesses involved in health care, private schools, research facilities, law firms, and repair shops.

Since the last half of the twentieth century, North Carolina has become known as a center for research on everything from high technology to chemicals. Much of the research is done at Research Triangle Park,

HOLLYWOOD EAST

In the past few decades film production has become big business in North Carolina, particularly in Wilmington. Today so many film companies and production crews are active in the area that it is known as Hollywood East. Such famous films as *Blue Velvet* and *Virus* have been filmed there. The area also provided the scenic setting for the once-popular television series *Dawson's Creek*.

So why has Wilmington become so appealing to film and television producers? "I guess Wilmington is as close as we can get to the American Dream. It's a real Norman Rockwell kind of town," said Mark Stricklin, director of the Wilmington Regional Film Commission, referring to the painter famous for his sentimental scenes of small-town life. "In this day and age, that's pretty attractive."

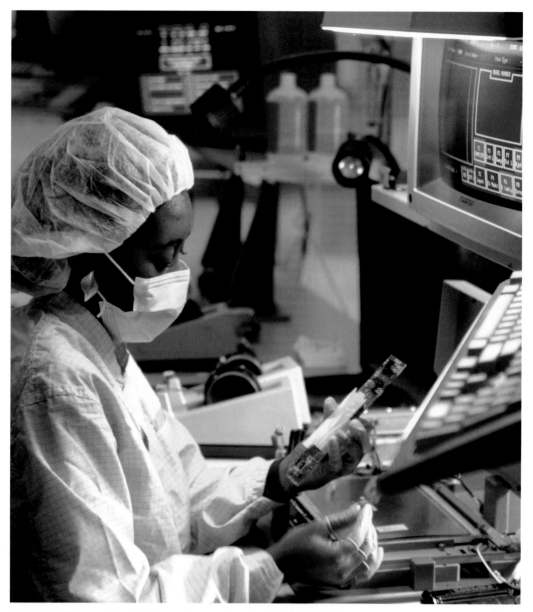

Research Triangle Park, located outside of Raleigh, has drawn hi-tech businesses, such as IBM, to the state.

located between Raleigh and Durham. The Research Triangle was founded in 1958 as a collaboration between Duke University, the University of North Carolina at Chapel Hill, North Carolina State University, and several local businesses. Today, Research Triangle houses the largest collection of research-based businesses in the country.

The third-largest sector of the service industry includes restaurants, hotels, and retail stores, such as those found in shopping malls. Both state and federal government businesses rank fourth in the service sector. Public schools, public hospitals, and military bases are included under government services.

The economic recession that hit the nation in 2008 and 2009 affected many of North Carolina's businesses. Though many businesspeople remained optimistic that the economy would turn around, there was no clear sign that this would happen quickly. People hoped, however, that by investing in the education of workers so they could take on the challenges of high-tech jobs, the state's economic outlook would improve. Many North Carolinians acknowledged that there was a need for change and were willing to take the steps necessary to help their state remain economically vibrant.

Chapter Six

From Mountain to Beach

North Carolina is a fascinating mix of dramatic peaks, white beaches, sleepy towns, and thriving cities. Let's take a quick tour of some of them.

THE MOUNTAINS

Western North Carolina's biggest attraction is the Blue Ridge Parkway. This scenic road snakes through the mountains from the Virginia state line in the north, all the way to the Tennessee border to the east. Cars creep along the parkway at a snail's pace as their passengers take in the breathtaking mountain views that spread out in every direction.

A popular stop is the spectacular Grandfather Mountain. The most exciting thing about it is the swinging bridge that connects two of its towering peaks. On clear days visitors who are brave enough to cross the bridge can gaze straight down into the valley that plunges below their feet. "I've been to Grandfather Mountain at least a dozen times over the years," says a store owner from Boone, "but I still feel the same fear and excitement every time I walk across that old bridge. You look out all

With more than 300 miles of unspoiled coast, it is easy to find the perfect beach along North Carolina's peaceful shore.

The Mile High Swinging Bridge on Grandfather Mountain, with a 228-foot suspension bridge that connects two peaks over an 80-foot drop, makes this a favorite spot of the more daring visitor.

around you in every direction, and you feel like you're floating on top of the world. It makes me feel dizzy just thinking about it."

Hidden away in the heart of the Great Smoky Mountains is the Cherokee Indian Reservation, the largest Indian reservation in the eastern United States. The reservation is the original hiding place of the Cherokee who escaped capture by federal troops in 1838. A highlight of the reservation is a re-created Cherokee village from the colonial period known as the Oconaluftee Indian Village. In it you can see miniature clay and log houses like those in which the Cherokee lived more than 250 years ago. You can also watch young Cherokee men demonstrate traditional hunting skills with blowguns and bows and arrows.

PLACES TO SEE

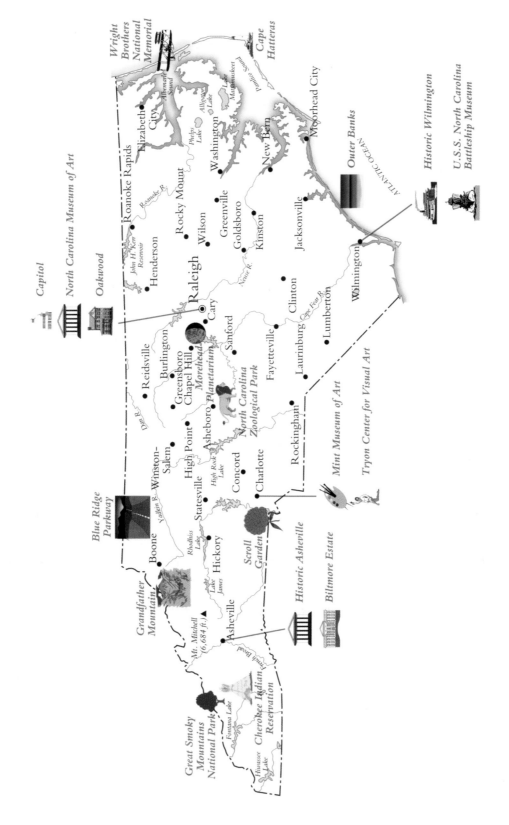

ASHEVILLE

Perched on the eastern rim of the Blue Ridge Mountains, Asheville is a rich blend of traditional and modern elements. Over the years it has been home to several of the state's most prominent citizens, including politician Zebulon B. Vance and novelist Thomas Wolfe. Vance was a popular governor and senator in the years following the Civil War. An enormous statue honoring his achievements is located in Pack Square, near the heart of downtown. A few blocks away, Wolfe's childhood home has been restored as a museum celebrating his life and work.

More than anything else Asheville is known for its splendid architecture. Several of Asheville's tall buildings date from the 1920s, when sharp angles and gleaming steel supports were popular. Erected in 1925, the fifteen-story Jackson Building was the city's first skyscraper. It still casts a dark shadow over the people strolling along Pack Square. Across from Pack Square the city hall was designed to resemble a mountain fortress. Completed in 1928, it is made of a colorful blend of marble, brick, and terra-cotta. Its architect, Douglas D. Ellington, reportedly designed the building's eight-sided roof to resemble the traditional headdress worn by American Indians from the region.

Asheville has long been a popular gathering place for people interested in bluegrass music and mountain folk art. Painters, wood carvers,

Western North Carolina's first skyscraper, the magnificent Jackson building, boasts fifteen stories of marble, brick, and terra-cotta.

and instrument makers sell their work in small stores throughout Asheville. And on most evenings musicians playing bluegrass and old-time mountain songs perform around the city. In recent years the area has begun to attract young people involved in more modern music and art. In the city's parks and public plazas experimental painters, musicians, and performance artists occasionally display their talent alongside traditional musicians and craftspeople. "It's really amazing, if you think about it," says a young classical musician who recently moved to the area, "that such a

Artists and performers offer tourist entertainment in Asheville's city parks.

small, seemingly isolated place could have room for so many types of people and so many forms of artistic expression. There's old-time music, performance art, rock and roll, jazz. It's all here in Asheville."

CHARLOTTE

Snuggled beneath the foothills of the Appalachian Mountains, Charlotte is North Carolina's largest city. It is filled with art galleries and museums. The Mint Museum of Art was the state's first museum to display classical European and American paintings and also features one of the nation's finest collections of pottery and porcelain. Another museum,

THE BILTMORE ESTATE

Outside of Asheville stands one of the state's most impressive landmarks, the lavish Biltmore Estate. Completed in 1895 for George Washington Vanderbilt of the famous shipping and railroad family, the estate took six years to build and was designed to rival the great country manors of Europe.

The largest and most expensive home ever built in the United States, the Biltmore House has 255 rooms covering more than 4 acres of floor space. In all, the mansion features thirty-four bedrooms, forty-three bathrooms, and sixty-five working fireplaces. It also has an indoor bowling alley and swimming pool. The grounds are as impressive as the manor itself, with 8,000 acres of forests and parks and a 75-acre garden.

"I think of the Biltmore House as one of North Carolina's finest treasures," says a Durham resident. "It's a fairy tale house of wealth and splendor and pleasure. Everything there is larger than life, from the bookcases to the portraits to the staircases. The first time I saw it decorated for Christmas, I felt like I was in a dream. My eyes could not take in all the beauty."

TEN LARGEST CITIES

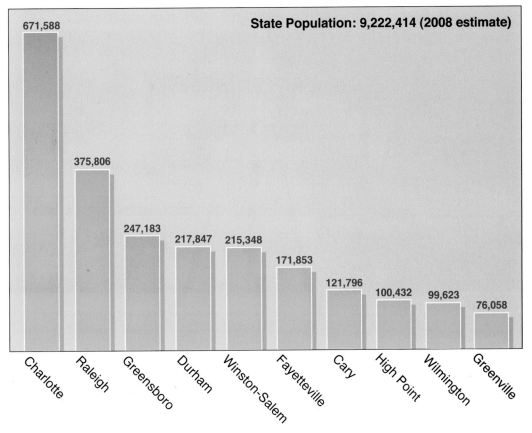

State Population: 9,222,414 (2008 estimate)

- Charlotte: 671,588
- Raleigh: 375,806
- Greensboro: 247,183
- Durham: 217,847
- Winston-Salem: 215,348
- Fayetteville: 171,853
- Cary: 121,796
- High Point: 100,432
- Wilmington: 99,623
- Greenville: 76,058

By Hand, focuses on handcrafted work by folk artists and potters from throughout the Southeast. The Tryon Center for Visual Art, located in a beautifully restored church building in the city's historic district, features a spectacular collection of contemporary art.

Daniel Stowe Botanical Garden is one of the South's largest and most colorful botanical gardens. It is located in nearby Belmont.

Seasonal flowers fill the Canal Garden, one of Daniel Stowe Botanical Garden's most popular rooms.

Highlights of the sprawling grounds include the Scroll Garden, which is filled with butterflies and birds, and the Canal Garden, which is filled with amazing tropical flowers.

RALEIGH

In the heart of the Piedmont region is the state capital, Raleigh. The capitol occupies two entire tree-lined blocks at the heart of the city's downtown. With its enormous columns and dome, it is widely regarded as one of the nation's outstanding examples of Greek Revival architecture. The governor's mansion sits at the edge of a historic neighborhood of elaborate nineteenth-century homes. U.S. president Franklin Delano

Roosevelt once described it as "the most beautiful governor's residence in America."

Raleigh is known as a city of parks, gardens, and nature trails. The metropolitan area has 150 major parks. Not far from downtown, Pullen Park features a carousel, a miniature train ride, and paddleboats. During the spring and summer Shelley Lake is filled with sailboats and pedal boats as runners circle the Greenway trail bordering the water. "There's not a better place in this country to live and raise a family," brags a government employee in Raleigh. "The whole area is covered with dogwoods and pine trees, and in the spring and summer the roads and sidewalks are lined with flowers. And you never had a problem finding a place to play ball with your kids or have a picnic with your family. The whole city feels like it was made for people to live in, and that's something you just don't see that much of these days."

The architectural details of North Carolina's Capitol, including the columns and ornamental honeysuckle atop the dome, were carefully patterned after features of Greek temples.

WILMINGTON

Located near the state's southeastern corner, Wilmington is North Carolina's leading seaport and one of its fastest-growing cities. A major part of Wilmington's appeal lies in the preservation of its colorful history. Historic downtown Wilmington features trolleys and vintage riverboats docked in the harbor. With its 230 blocks of restored buildings and

There is truly something for everyone in the downtown historic district of Wilmington, North Carolina, such as a horse-drawn carriage ride.

landmarks, it is one of the largest historic districts in the nation. Visitors can either tour the area by foot or hitch a ride in a horse-drawn carriage.

Docked on the Cape Fear River is another piece of history, the USS *North Carolina* Memorial. Nicknamed the Showboat, the enormous ship was an important part of every major sea battle in the Pacific Ocean during World War II.

THE OUTER BANKS

Most of the coastline north of Wilmington is guarded by the narrow string of islands known as the Outer Banks. The islands of the Outer Banks are connected to the mainland by a series of towering bridges that sweep up from one shore and down onto the other. Most people who visit the area come to see the snowy white beaches.

North of Wilmington the jagged beach of Cape Hatteras juts out into the Atlantic Ocean like a giant elbow. Known as the Graveyard of the Atlantic, the cape has been the site of countless boating accidents over the years. Time and time again boaters have ventured too close to the shore and lost control in the powerful tides. In 1870, Cape Hatteras Lighthouse, one of the largest on the East Coast, was erected at the tip of the cape to warn ships approaching the shore. Today this magnificent brick structure is painted in stripes of black and white and rises 180 feet above the water.

Farther north on the Outer Banks is the hilly stretch of beach known as Nags Head. Visitors to the area enjoy climbing to the top of the enormous dunes, which provides spectacular views of the blue, white-capped water of the Atlantic.

A few miles north are the beaches of Kitty Hawk and Kill Devil Hills. A 91-foot monument at the top of Kill Devil Hills marks the site where the Wright brothers made the world's first controlled motorized flight in 1903. You can also visit replicas of the hangar and workshop where the Wright brothers built and repaired their airplanes. Today, visitors fly kites instead of airplanes in the powerful winds that blow across the beach.

"There's so much to see in North Carolina," says a recent visitor to Kill Devil Hills. "There's so much history and so much beauty right here side by side. When I was growing up, folks used to argue about which was the best—the mountains or the ocean. But if you're honest with yourself, there's really no way you can make a choice. You just have to see them both—and everything that's in between. That's the only way you can really get to know North Carolina."

THE FLAG: *The right-hand side of the state flag features a red bar above a white bar. On the left is a blue vertical stripe with a white star and the letters N and C in the center. Above the star is a scroll bearing the date May 20, 1775, the day Mecklenburg County is said to have declared independence from Britain. Below it is a scroll bearing the date April 12, 1776, the day North Carolina agreed that delegates to the Continental Congress should vote for American independence.*

THE SEAL: *The state seal was adopted in 1971. On the left a figure representing liberty holds a scroll bearing the word* Constitution. *On the right a seated figure represents plenty. Below them is the state motto in Latin:* Esse quam videri *(To be, rather than to seem). The dates that appear on the flag also appear on the state seal.*

State Survey

Statehood: November 21, 1789

Origin of Name: The region was named *Carolana*, which means "land of Charles" in Latin, after King Charles I of England

Nickname: Tar Heel State

Capital: Raleigh

Motto: To Be, Rather Than to Seem

Bird: Cardinal

Flower: Dogwood

Trees: Longleaf pine

Fish: Channel bass

Insect: Honeybee

Precious Stone: Emerald

Reptile: Eastern box turtle

Rock: Granite

Shell: Scotch bonnet

Cardinal

Dogwood

THE OLD NORTH STATE

"The Old North State" was adopted as the official song of North Carolina in 1927.

Highest Point: 6,684 feet above sea level, at Mount Mitchell

Lowest Point: sea level along the coast

Area: 53,819 square miles

Greatest Distance North to South: 188 miles

Greatest Distance East to West: 499 miles

Bordering States: Virginia to the north, Tennessee to the west, South Carolina and Georgia to the south

Hottest Recorded Temperature: 110 °F at Fayetteville on August 21, 1983

Coldest Recorded Temperature: –34 °F at Mount Mitchell on January 21, 1985

Average Annual Precipitation: 50 inches

Major Rivers: Cape Fear, Catawba, Little Tennessee, Nantahala, Neuse, Roanoke, Tar, Yadkin

Major Lakes: Fontana, High Rock, Mattamuskeet, New, Norman, Phelps

Trees: cedar, cypress, gum, hickory, loblolly pine, maple, oak, pine, tulip

Wild Plants: azalea, camellia, dogwood, orchid, pitcher plant, redbud, rhododendron, sundew

Animals: beaver, black bear, dolphin, fox, otter, rabbit, raccoon, skunk, white-tailed deer

Birds: Carolina wren, duck, goose, mockingbird, mourning dove, partridge, swan, woodcock

Fish: bass, bluegill, crappie, flounder, marlin, menhaden, sailfish, sturgeon, sunfish, trout

Black bear

Endangered Animals: Appalachian elktoe, Cape Fear shiner, Carolina heelsplitter, Carolina northern flying squirrel, dwarf wedgemussel, eastern puma, finback whale, humpback whale, Indiana bat, Kemp's ridley sea turtle, leatherback sea turtle, littlewing pearlymussel, red wolf, red-cockaded woodpecker, right whale, roseate tern, Saint Francis' satyr butterfly, shortnose sturgeon, sperm whale, spruce-fir moss spider, Tar River spiny mussel, Virginia big-eared bat, West Indian manatee

Red-cockaded woodpecker

Endangered Plants: American chaffseed, bunched arrowhead, Canby's dropwort, Cooley's meadowrue, green pitcher plant, harperella, Michaux's sumac, mountain sweet pitcher plant, pondberry, Roan Mountain bluet, rock gnome lichen, rough-leaved loosestrife, Schweinitz's sunflower, small-anthered bittercress, smooth coneflower, spreading avens, white irisette

TIMELINE

North Carolina History

1400s Cherokee, Hatteras, Catawba, Chowanoc, Tuscarora, and other Indian tribes live in what is now North Carolina.

1524 Giovanni da Verrazano becomes the first European to explore the North Carolina coast.

1540 Spaniard Hernando de Soto becomes the first white man to cross North Carolina's southwestern mountains.

1585 The first English colony in what is now the United States is established at Roanoke Island.

1587 Virginia Dare of Roanoke Island becomes the first English child born in America.

1650 North Carolina's first permanent white settlement is established near Albemarle Sound.

1705 Bath, North Carolina's first town, is incorporated; North Carolina's first school opens near Elizabeth City.

1711 Tuscarora Indians attack white settlements, killing hundreds of people and marking the beginning of the Tuscarora War.

1712 North Carolina and South Carolina become separate colonies.

1751 The *North Carolina Gazette*, the region's first newspaper, begins publication.

1775–1783 The American Revolution is fought.

1789 North Carolina becomes the twelfth state.

1795 The University of North Carolina becomes the first public university to begin holding classes.

1861 The Civil War begins; North Carolina secedes from the Union.

1871 North Carolinian William W. Holden becomes the nation's first governor to be impeached.

1903 Wilbur and Orville Wright make the world's first successful motorized airplane flight at Kill Devil Hills.

1917 The United States enters World War I.

1935 Construction begins on the Blue Ridge Parkway, a scenic route linking national parks in Virginia and North Carolina.

1941–1945 Nearly 370,000 North Carolinians serve in the armed forces during World War II.

1959 North Carolina Research Triangle Park, run by three universities to serve industry, opens. It brings economic prosperity to Durham, Raleigh, and Chapel Hill.

1960 Four black students start the sit-in movement at a lunch counter in Greensboro to protest racial segregation.

1971 The state's third and present constitution goes into effect.

1972 Jesse Helms becomes the first Republican from North Carolina elected to the U.S. Senate since 1903.

1989 Hurricane Hugo strikes North Carolina, devastating the state as far inland as Charlotte and the foothills of the mountains.

1994 The Raleigh-Durham area is ranked the best place in the United States to live by *Money* magazine.

1996 Hurricane Fran pounds North Carolina, causing $1 billion in damage.

2004 Hurricane Isabel smashes into the Outer Banks.

2005 The state legislature approves the creation of a lottery to help fund education.

2008 Beverly Perdue becomes North Carolina's first female governor.

ECONOMY

Agricultural Products: apples, blueberries, catfish, chickens, corn, hogs, milk, peaches, peanuts, soybeans, strawberries, sweet potatoes, tobacco, turkeys

Manufactured Products: carpeting, chemicals, cigarettes, cloth, computers, construction equipment, food products, furniture, hosiery, telephone equipment, yarn

Natural Resources: crushed stone, feldspar, fish, sand and gravel, shellfish

Strawberries

Business and Trade: banking, insurance, real estate, research, tourism, wholesale and retail trade

North Carolina Azalea Festival Each spring, when North Carolina's azaleas burst into bloom, Wilmington celebrates with a long weekend of garden tours, concerts, and a grand parade.

North Carolina Azalea Festival

Ham and Yam Festival More sweet potatoes (also known as yams) are grown in Johnston County than any other county in the United States. In April the town of Smithfield serves them up in style with another North Carolina specialty, home-cured country ham.

Shad Festival Every April the town of Grifton throws a party in honor of the shad, a small, bony fish that swims in a creek at the edge of town.

North Carolina Blackbeard Festival The most notorious pirate ever to torment the eastern seaboard takes center stage at this May celebration in Morehead City. Special events include a re-created pirate battle, a treasure hunt, and a Blackbeard look-alike contest.

Fossil Festival Visitors to Aurora get a free guided tour of nearby fossil beds during this May event. Guests can dig for their own fossils or examine those on display in town, along with a wide array of minerals.

Highland Games and Gathering of the Clans Grandfather Mountain hosts the country's largest Scottish games in July, with traditional dancing and piping, sheepdog-herding demonstrations, and athletic contests.

Mountain Dance and Folk Festival The best musicians and dancers in the Appalachians perform at this August festival in Asheville.

Benson Mule Days Each September you'll see Benson's most stubborn animals perform all kinds of amazing feats, from leaping tall fences

Highland Games and Gathering of the Clans

to pulling massive loads. The best of the bunch leads a parade of two thousand mules and horses through the center of town.

Cherokee Indian Fair Each October American Indians celebrate their heritage during a five-day festival in Cherokee. Activities include stickball games, archery and blowgun contests, and traditional dancing.

John Blue Cotton Festival Laurinburg takes a step back in time during the second weekend in October, with exhibits including a mule-driven cotton gin and a grist mill. Don't miss the old-fashioned Sunday church service.

Woolly Worm Festival Legend has it that you can tell whether a harsh winter is coming by counting the stripes on the woolly worm, a fuzzy black and reddish brown caterpillar. But since each caterpillar is different, forecasts aren't always consistent. Every fall Banner Elk holds a woolly worm race to see which caterpillar should be the final authority.

Core Sound Decoy Festival The art of carving wooden duck decoys has a long history in coastal North Carolina. December brings hundreds of artists and collectors to Harkers Island, where locals celebrate the craft with carving competitions, a loon-calling contest, and a fair featuring new and antique decoys.

STATE STARS

David Brinkley (1920–2003) was a prominent television journalist and commentator. In the 1960s Brinkley became a household name as co-anchor, with Chet Huntley, of television's *Huntley-Brinkley Report*. He later hosted his own news show, *This Week with David Brinkley*. Brinkley, who was born in Wilmington, won ten Emmy Awards and two Peabody Awards for outstanding television journalism.

John Coltrane (1926–1967), one of the world's greatest saxophonists, was born in Hamlet. As a young man Coltrane played sax in the style of the legendary Charlie Parker, but by the late 1950s he had developed a way of playing all his own, featuring intense, elaborate solos and rapid improvisation. Brilliant on both alto and tenor sax, Coltrane also gave the soprano sax its first major role in jazz. His most famous recordings include *A Love Supreme* and *My Favorite Things*.

David Brinkley

Cecil B. DeMille (1881–1959) was an influential film producer. In 1913 DeMille helped make Hollywood's first feature-length movie, *The Squaw Man*. DeMille later directed such sweeping epics as *The Greatest Show on Earth*, for which he won an Academy Award, and the hugely popular *The Ten Commandments*. DeMille spent most of his childhood in Washington, North Carolina.

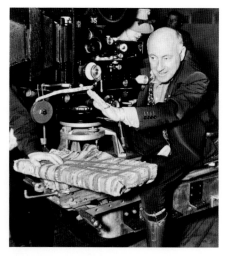

Cecil B. DeMille

Elizabeth Dole (1936–   ), a leading Republican politician, has held posts under six different presidents, including secretary of labor under Ronald Reagan and secretary of labor under George H. W. Bush. In 1991 Dole became president of the American Red Cross, and in 2000 she campaigned for the Republican presidential nomination. Dole was born in Salisbury. She was North Carolina's first female U.S. senator, holding office from 2003 until 2009.

James Buchanan Duke (1856–1925) of Durham turned his family's tobacco-processing business into one of the country's biggest industries. Duke used new technology and advertising to make cigarette manufacturing profitable, then bought up competitors to create a vast tobacco empire. When he died, he left a trust fund to Durham's Trinity College, now known as Duke University.

Elizabeth Dole

Roberta Flack (1937–   ), a church organist's daughter from Black Mountain, hit the top of the pop charts in 1972 with her smooth rendition of the song "The First Time Ever I Saw Your Face." Flack's velvety voice and elegant style on ballads like "Killing Me Softly with His Song" and "Set the Night to Music" made a huge impact on popular music in the 1970s and 1980s. In 2008 she put out a new CD called *At Her Best: Live.*

Ava Gardner (1922–1990) was a sultry, glamorous film actress. Born near Smithfield, Gardner was discovered by Hollywood after her brother-in-law, a photographer, displayed pictures of her in the window of his New York studio. She went on to play the romantic lead in such classic films as *Show Boat, One Touch of Venus,* and *On the Beach.*

Ava Gardner

Richard Gatling (1818–1903) invented the Gatling gun, one of the first machine guns to be effective in war. As a young man he invented a machine for sowing wheat. He went on to develop a series of mechanical devices, including the gun that bears his name. The Gatling gun, which could fire close to three hundred rounds per minute, was widely used by the U.S. Army in the late nineteenth century.

Roberta Flack

Billy Graham (1918–), a native of Charlotte, is one of America's most famous preachers and a leading spokesman for conservative Christianity. Graham went on his first major preaching tour of the United States and Europe in 1949. He has since traveled the globe many times, captivating listeners with his fiery, eloquent sermons. In 2005 Graham made an appearance at the ground-breaking ceremony for a library in his honor in Charlotte.

Andy Griffith (1926–), who grew up in Mount Airy, was the longtime star of *The Andy Griffith Show*, a 1960s television series about life in the fictional North Carolina town of Mayberry. He later played a cool-headed lawyer in the television series *Matlock*. In 2005 Griffith received the Presidential Medal of Freedom for his life's work.

Mia Hamm (1972–), who makes her home in Chapel Hill, is one of the most talented female soccer players in the world. In 1987, at age fifteen, Hamm became the youngest person ever to join the U.S. national women's soccer team. She later led North Carolina's Tar Heels to four national championships and became the top scorer in the National Collegiate Athletic Association (NCAA) women's soccer history. Hamm's fast and accurate playing style helped the U.S. national team win the Women's World Cup in 1991 and 1999. She retired from the sport in 2004, and in 2007 she was inducted into the National Soccer Hall of Fame.

Mia Hamm

Jesse Helms (1921– 2008) was a U.S. senator from North Carolina from 1973 to 2003. Born in Monroe, Helms worked as a journalist and a television executive in Raleigh before entering politics. Known for his outspoken conservatism on social issues, in 1995 he became chairman of the influential Senate Foreign Relations Committee.

O. Henry (1862–1910) is the pen name of William Sydney Porter, a short story writer famous for his surprise endings. Although he turned to writing late in life, this Greensboro native became one of the most popular writers of his generation, publishing hundreds of short stories during his career. Today, his contribution to the short story is remembered with the O. Henry Memorial Award, given each year to the writers of the best American short stories.

O. Henry

Andrew Johnson (1808–1875), a native of Raleigh, was the seventeenth president of the United States. Johnson entered politics after moving to Tennessee, where he became famous for his powerful speeches in defense of the working class. He was elected vice president shortly before President Abraham Lincoln was assassinated in 1865. As Lincoln's successor, Johnson quickly became unpopular with northern politicians, who thought he was too forgiving toward the South after the Civil War. In 1868 he became the first president to be tried for impeachment, which means the U.S. House of Representatives voted that the Senate should hold a trial to decide whether he should be removed from office. The Senate, however, voted not to remove him.

Michael Jordan (1963–) is widely regarded as the greatest basketball player of all time. Born in Brooklyn, New York, and raised in Wilmington, he played basketball for the University of North Carolina for three years before joining the Chicago Bulls. During his twelve-year professional career, he led the Bulls to six championships, and his charismatic personality and spectacular shooting made basketball popular worldwide.

Charles Kuralt (1934–1997) was an award-winning journalist whose reports on small-town America charmed television audiences for more than thirty years. He won three Peabody Awards and ten Emmys for his programs *On the Road with Charles Kuralt* and *Sunday Morning*. Kuralt was born in Wilmington.

Sugar Ray Leonard (1956–), one of the most talented boxers of his generation, won five world titles, beating his opponents in the welterweight, super welterweight, and middleweight classes. Leonard won the gold medal in the light welterweight division in the 1976 Olympics. He is a native of Wilmington.

Sugar Ray Leonard

Dolley Madison (1768–1849) was one of the most celebrated first ladies in U.S. history. Born in

Guilford County, she became active in Washington, D.C., society after marrying congressman James Madison in 1794. During Madison's presidency, from 1809 to 1817, she charmed the nation's capital with her Wednesday receptions, in which politicians, diplomats, and the public came together for an evening of socializing that eased political tensions.

John Merrick (1859–1919), a successful businessman, was born into slavery in Clinton and was brought up without formal schooling. After years of hard work in construction and shoe shining, he opened a barber shop in Durham and soon became a leader in the black business community. In 1898 he helped found the North Carolina Mutual Life Insurance Company in Durham, soon to become the nation's largest African-American–owned business.

Thelonious Monk (1917–1982) was a jazz pianist who, along with saxophonist Charlie Parker and trumpeter Dizzy Gillespie, helped create the fast, complex bebop style. Marked by uneven rhythms and strange sounds, Monk's music was so unusual that during his early years, jazz lovers sometimes thought he couldn't play well. It wasn't until the mid–1950s that he gained recognition as a groundbreaking pianist and composer. Today, his haunting melodies, notably "'Round Midnight," "Evidence," and "Misterioso," are among the most admired in jazz. Monk was born in Rocky Mount.

Edward R. Murrow (1908–1965) was a highly respected radio and television journalist. A Greensboro native, Murrow joined the CBS news team in 1935 and first gained acclaim for his on-the-scenes reporting during World War II. After the war he developed the radio program *Hear It Now* and later the television program *See It Now*, both of which dealt with controversial issues. In 1954 Murrow caused a sensation on his show when he took on Senator Joseph McCarthy's anti-communist crusade.

Richard Petty (1937–) is one of the greatest stock car drivers in racing history. Born in Randleman, Petty caught the racing bug from his father, stock car Hall of Famer Lee Petty. Richard eventually became his sport's all-time champion, with seven driver titles and two hundred career wins.

Richard Petty

James K. Polk (1795– 1849), the eleventh president of the United States, believed the nation was destined to expand west to the Pacific Ocean. His belief was realized in 1848 during his presidency, when the United States acquired California and much of the Southwest at the end of the Mexican War. Polk was born in Mecklenburg County.

Nina Simone (1933–2003) was a
singer, songwriter, and pianist from
Tryon. Simone recorded her first
hit, the George Gershwin song "I
Loves You Porgy," in the late 1950s.
She used her deep voice to sing
everything from gospel and jazz to
blues and folk.

Doc Watson (1923–   ) is a blues
musician known for his brilliance
on the acoustic guitar. Born in
Stoney Fork and raised in Deep
Gap, Arthel "Doc" Watson lost
his vision before he was one year
old. After learning to play guitar
as a teenager, he devoted himself

Nina Simone

to playing the music he grew up with, from country hits to old-time
fiddle tunes. Watson earned widespread acclaim after the release of his
album *Doc Watson* in 1964. Since then he has been honored with five
Grammy Awards and a National Medal of the Arts.

Thomas Wolfe (1900–1938) is a writer best known for four novels that
paint a vivid portrait of American life in the early twentieth century.
Wolf's *Look Homeward, Angel*; *Of Time and the River*; *The Web and
the Rock*; and *You Can't Go Home Again* are set against the backdrop
of his native North Carolina. Wolfe was born in Asheville.

Ocracoke Island (Ocracoke) This long strip of land about 30 miles off North Carolina's shore boasts quiet towns and beautiful sandy beaches. The pirate Blackbeard once hid out among the rocks along its western shore.

Duke Homestead and Tobacco Museum (Durham) Historic displays tell the story of the tobacco industry at the home of American Tobacco Company founder, Washington Duke.

Cherokee Indian Reservation (Cherokee) American-Indian history and traditions come to life at the Museum of the Cherokee Indian. During the summer, tribe members demonstrate traditional crafts at Oconaluftee Indian Village, built to look like a Cherokee town of the 1700s.

Cherokee Indian Reservation

Battleship *North Carolina* Memorial

Grandfather Mountain (Linville) Shaped like the face of an old man, this
rocky peak features a swinging bridge a mile high that links two peaks.

Battleship *North Carolina* Memorial (Wilmington) One of America's
most famous naval ships is docked on the Cape Fear River in
Wilmington. The USS *North Carolina* fought in every major battle
in the Pacific during World War II.

Chimney Rock (Chimney Rock) A trip to the top of this dramatic rock formation in Rutherford County guarantees dazzling views of the Blue Ridge Mountains.

Roanoke Island (Roanoke) The first two English settlements in the United States were established here, in 1585 and 1587. The second mysteriously disappeared. In Manteo an outdoor musical drama called *The Last Colony* vividly tells the tale.

Jockey's Ridge State Park (Nags Head) Giant dunes make this seaside park look like the Sahara desert, with its mountains of shifting sands. Strong winds make it a popular spot for hang gliding.

Jockey's Ridge State Park

Chimney Rock

Wright Brothers National Memorial (Kill Devil Hills) A 60-foot granite monument marks the spot where Orville and Wilbur Wright took flight and made history for the first time. Inside the visitors' center is a life-size model of their original plane.

Old Salem (Winston-Salem) The architecture of the colonial era is beautifully preserved in this restored village, founded in 1766.

Croatan National Forest (New Bern) The lakes and bogs of this 157,000-acre woods are crowded with such insect-eating plants as the sundew, the pitcher plant, and the Venus flytrap.

Biltmore Estate (Asheville) Millionaire George Vanderbilt once entertained guests in this 255-room chateau. Today it is the largest home in America, and its formal gardens are open for public tours.

Morehead Planetarium (Chapel Hill) Stars and planets move across a giant dome at this planetarium, where astronauts once practiced navigating by the stars.

Nantahala Gorge (Bryson City) The name of this narrow canyon in the mountains means "Land of the Noonday Sun." The gorge is so deep and narrow that the sun only peeps in around noon.

North Carolina Museum of Art (Raleigh) This renowned art museum displays a vast array of American and European art.

Great Smoky Mountains National Park (Cherokee) About five hundred black bears thrive in the country's most popular national park, which straddles the border between North Carolina and Tennessee.

Nantahala Gorge

Cape Hatteras Lighthouse (Buxton) Built in 1870, this black-and-white–striped landmark was moved 2,900 feet inland in 1999 to save it from being washed away. It guards Cape Hatteras, which has such treacherous waters, it is known as the Graveyard of the Atlantic.

Blue Ridge Parkway (Asheville) America's best-loved scenic drive meanders along the top of the Blue Ridge Mountains, offering breathtaking views to drivers traveling along it.

Blue Ridge Parkway

Cape Hatteras Lighthouse

North Carolina Zoological Park (Asheboro) Animals from across North America and Africa can be seen at one of the nation's largest zoos.

Bentonville Battleground State Historic Site (Four Oaks) The last major Civil War battle fought in North Carolina took place near Bentonville. Visitors can tour the farmhouse that served as a field hospital during the fighting.

North Carolina Zoological Park

Reed Gold Mine State Historic Site

Reed Gold Mine State Historic Site (Stanfield) America's first gold rush was launched by a twelve-year-old boy named Conrad Reed in Cabarrus County. You can try your own luck searching for the precious metal near the spot where his family grew rich by panning 115 pounds of gold.

Tobacco Farm Life Museum (Kenly) This restored farmstead and museum offers a glimpse of farm life from the late nineteenth century through the 1950s.

FUN FACTS

At 411 feet tall, Whitewater Falls in Transylvania County is the highest waterfall on the East Coast.

The University of North Carolina was the first public university in the United States to open its doors.

Virginia Dare, born in Roanoke in 1587, was the first English child born in America.

Baseball legend Babe Ruth hit his first professional home run in Fayetteville on March 7, 1914.

The Biltmore Estate in Asheville is the largest private house in the world, with thirty-four bedrooms, forty-three bathrooms, and sixty-five fireplaces.

The Cape Hatteras Lighthouse is the tallest lighthouse in the United States.

Find Out More

To find out more about North Carolina, check your local library or bookstore for these titles.

GENERAL STATE BOOKS

Alex, Nan. *North Carolina* (From Sea to Shining Sea). New York: Children's Press, 2008.

Cannavale, Matthew C. *Voices from Colonial America: North Carolina 1524–1776*. Washington, DC: National Geographic Children's Books, 2007.

Haberle, Susan E. *The North Carolina Colony* (Fact Finders: American Colonies). Mankato, MN: Capstone Press, 2006.

Mayr, Diane. *North Carolina* (Portraits of the States). Strongsville, OH: Gareth Stevens Publishing, 2005.

SPECIAL INTERST BOOKS

Boyd, Bentley. *Tar Heel Tales*. Williamsburg, VA: Chester Comix, 2005.

Goldman, Phyllis Barkas. *North Carolina African American History & Culture*. Greensboro, NC: Allosaurus Publishers, 2007.

WEBSITES

50states.com: North Carolina, A Better Place to Be

www.50states.com/ncarolin.htm

This site provides a long list of links on North Carolina history, government, geography, and symbols, including facts about the state and brief biographies of famous North Carolinians.

Official Website of the State of North Carolina

www.ncgov.com/

This site provides links to lists of government officials, a kids' page, and descriptions of places to visit.

State Library of North Carolina

statelibrary.dcr.state.nc.us/

The official website of the State Library of North Carolina includes a thorough introduction to the government, history, geography, and famous people of the state.

Storytelling of the North Carolina Native Americans

www.ibiblio.org/storytelling/

This website was created by the University of North Carolina and provides links to histories as told by three different tribes, as well as to videotapes of native storytellers creating their art.

Index

Page numbers in **boldface** are illustrations and charts.

David Shirley has written a dozen books for young people, including *Mississippi* and *Alabama* in the Celebrate the States series. He is a former resident of Raleigh and Wake Forest, North Carolina, and now lives in Brooklyn, New York. Raised in Tupelo, Mississippi, Shirley spends his spare time collecting beetles and writing country music.

Joyce Hart has a long history with North Carolina, though she has never lived there. When her sons were very young, she took them to the Outer Banks each summer to enjoy the ocean and the sand dunes. Her eldest son now has his own family and lives outside of Raleigh. During the summers he now takes her to the beach with his family. Hart has written more than thirty books for students. She lives on the West Coast, outside of Seattle.